Missouri's Black Heritage

Missouri's Black Heritage

Lorenzo J. Greene
Gary R. Kremer
Anthony F. Holland

Foreword by
Julius K. Hunter

FORUM PRESS

Published simultaneously in Canada

Printed in the United States of America

Library of Congress Catalog Card Number: 79-54887

ISBN: 0-88273-115-7

Cover and Design by Jerry Moore and Janet Moody

Maps by Laura Poracsky

To our wives and children

Preface

Missouri's Black Heritage, with a foreword by Julius Hunter, represents our effort to provide an account of a neglected aspect of the state's past. Missouri, like the nation as a whole, is the product of the efforts of diverse races, nationalities, and creeds. People from all backgrounds have mixed their heritage, blood, brawn, and brains to create a home for themselves and their children. Students living in a multiracial society in which the largest single minority group is Afro-American should understand the obstacles against which blacks have had to fight. They should also understand that despite these obstacles, many black people have achieved success.

For generations, an ignorance of the value and contributions of black Americans bred fear and hatred. Children were taught that blacks deserved second-class citizenship. Such a position for blacks was sanctioned by law at the highest levels of American society. Black and white children alike were led to believe that black people had made little or no contribution to American civilization and that the treatment they had received from white society was justified by alleged black inferiority and depravity. The net result was that white children grew up with an unjustified sense of superiority, while black children nursed a feeling of inferiority. The barbarities of the slave ships were said to be justified because at least the trip to the New World removed the African from the so-called savage influences of the "Dark Continent." Likewise, it was argued that while slavery was a harsh institution, it was justified because it exposed the "heathen" to the possibility of salvation in the heavenly kingdom of the Christian God, providing the slave was content and happy in his bondage.

Perhaps one of the most remarkable things about the black experience in America is that black people have survived despite the treatment they have received. Indeed, they have more than survived—they have played a vital role in structuring the American present. It is crucial, therefore, to understand their past.

Throughout their history black people have variously asked that they be called by different names: Colored Americans, Negroes, Afro-Americans, and many others. Because we are writing in the decade of the seventies, we have accepted what appears to us to be the common contemporary term by which the majority of Americans of African descent prefer to be known: black Americans or simply blacks.

In writing this book, we accept the responsibility for the selection and interpretation of facts as well as any errors which may exist. We are indebted to our students and colleagues at Lincoln University for their interest and assistance. We are particularly grateful to the Ethnic Studies Center for its financial support and to Darryl C. Cook for his research assistance. We wish also to acknowledge the helpful suggestions from the following individuals who reviewed portions of the manuscript prior to publication: George A. Rawick, University of Missouri—St. Louis; William E. Foley, Central Missouri State University; Warren E. Solomon, State Department of Education; Edward Beasley, Penn Valley Community College; J. Christopher Schnell, Southeast Missouri State University; Enid Muskkin of the Black Motivational Center of Kansas City; Barbara Woods, Director of Black Studies, St. Louis University; Dominic Capeci, Southwest Missouri State University; Nancy Fields, Harris-Stowe State College; Carolyn Dorsey, Director of Black Studies, University of Missouri—Columbia; Julia Davis, retired St. Louis teacher; Russell Sackreiter, a social studies teacher in the Columbia Public Schools; Ellen Martin, Jefferson City Senior High School, who shared some of our material with her Missouri history classes, and Lorenzo Thomas Greene. Additionally Frederic A. Youngs, Jr., of Louisiana State University and Donald Ewalt, Jr., of Lincoln University read the manuscript in its entirety and made many useful comments. The staffs of the following libraries have also been quite helpful: the State Historical Society of Missouri (Columbia), the Missouri Historical Society (St. Louis), and the Inman E. Page Library of Lincoln University. The *St. Louis Amer-*

ican graciously opened its valuable photo files to us, as did the *Kansas City Star,* the *St. Louis Post-Dispatch,* and the *St. Louis Globe-Democrat.* Also, the Reverend James Blair of Kansas City assisted in the search for photos. Lastly, we wish to express our appreciation to the staff of Forum Press for assistance in the publication of this book, especially to Erby M. Young and W. A. Welsh who recognized the need for *Missouri's Black Heritage* and who encouraged and guided us every step of the way.

Contents

Foreword

Julius Hunter

The state of Missouri provides an excellent focal point for an examination of black history in the United States. Missouri has been a mirror reflection of the nation as it displayed its confusion, indifference, guilt, cruelty, pride, subterfuge, embarrassment, benevolence, and sympathy in handling the issue of how blacks should and would be treated.

The issue of slavery caused Missouri a great deal of schizophrenia even before it was admitted to the Union, and treatment of its black citizens has caused Missouri a great deal of trauma after statehood was achieved in 1821. Missouri had gone through the process of becoming a state along with Alabama, Arkansas, Louisiana, and Mississippi. Such company entitled—or destined—Missouri to have some identity with the "Lower South." But, with Kentucky, Missouri at times tried to be a buffer to the entire Ohio and Upper Mississippi valleys. What's more, Missouri held tightly to its relationship with the southern states while trying to maintain the geographical and ideological posture as "Gateway to the West."

In 1818—just three years before statehood—the Missouri Territory watched its border state to the east, Illinois, firmly ban slavery by specific law. In fact, Missouri's geographical location must have caused its slaveowners many sleepless nights. It must have been difficult to hold on to slaves while being surrounded on three sides by the free states of Illinois, Iowa, and Kansas.

In the same year that neighboring Illinois banned slavery, the Missouri Territory demonstrated its understanding of the horrors of living in bondage by providing a penalty of "death without benefit of clergy" for selling a free person—blacks included—into slavery if the seller clearly knew that the person sold was, indeed, free. There are more examples of Missouri's Jekyll and Hyde approach to slavery. In 1819 Missouri Territory lobbyists and other Southern forces helped defeat a proposal in the U. S. Senate to free all slaves in the soon-to-be-admitted state when the slaves reached the age of twenty-five. Chalk up a victory for pro-slavery forces. But then, in 1820, the same Missouri legislative forces allowed the new state constitution to include a provision for a trial by jury for slaves, equal punishment for slaves and whites for like crimes, and, astonishingly, court-assigned counsel for the slave's defense. Before that beneficence is given too much praise, we should remember that the year before this kindly paper act, Missouri Territory lawmakers made it a crime to teach blacks—slave or free—to read. The General Assembly reinforced that edict with stronger legislation in 1847 and didn't get around to repealing the law until 1870.

To further compound the contradictory approaches to treatment for its black residents, Missouri had to make its actions compatible with those of higher forces. When the Missouri legislature gave slaves the right to sue for freedom in 1824, the U. S. Supreme Court's 1857 ruling on the Dred Scott case reminded Missouri and the rest of the nation that black slaves were "not people of the United States and had no rights which a white man need respect." This Dred Scott decision must have thoroughly flabbergasted some Missourians who remembered the Vincent v. James Duncan case of 1830 in which the Supreme Court ruled that exportation of a slave to a free state gave him his freedom.

As the authors of this book point out, Missouri provided the nation with its first dress rehearsals for the Civil War. As early as 1856 abolitionist forces, armed with weapons and ideologies forged in the North, moved into Kansas. Pro-slavery forces, armed with weapons and credos manufactured in the South, moved into Missouri. Guerrilla warfare soon raged in the Kansas countryside and along the border until federal troops had to be called in to try to stop the killing. Those same troops would be fighting bigger battles in less than half a decade.

Then, too, an incident which happened here in Missouri can

be credited with de-romanticizing the image of "The Great Emancipator." In August of 1861 Abolitionist General John C. Fremont issued a declaration liberating all of Missouri's slaves. But Fremont's order was immediately countermanded by President Lincoln. Pressed by Northern newspapers to explain how he could reverse Fremont's magnanimous exercise of humanitarianism, Lincoln put the hard, cold facts on the table:

> If I could save the Union without freeing any slave, I would do it; and if I could save it by freeing all the slaves I would do it; and if I could do it (save the Union) by freeing some and leaving others alone, I would also do that. What I do about slavery and the colored race, I do because I believe it helps save this Union.

The "Emancipator" did not issue his Proclamation two years after the Fremont Missouri Emancipation for any other purpose except the attempted salvation of the Union. Lincoln's feelings on the matter of slaves could be judged by his actions. He refused the military services of two black Indiana units in August of 1862 but told the soldiers he could use them as laborers.

There were no opinion polls to sample Missouri's sympathies for Lincoln's views on the issue of slavery, but apparently the state was extremely well-tuned to Lincoln's sentiments. The state which so tenaciously held on to its slaves chose membership in the Union over and above its slave holdings. But the state still held onto its slaves. In fact, the potential secession of Missouri struck Lincoln as being a loss that would have been "too large for us."

The authors correct two common misconceptions which may be harbored by the casual student of Missouri's black history. Most Missouri slaves were not bound to the cotton fields, and not all the blacks who lived in the state during the slave years were held in bondage. Missouri's growing season kept cotton from becoming king in the state. Consequently, many of Missouri's slaves were put to a variety of less binding, more creative tasks. Those slaves who were not denigrated mentally and physically by the cotton fields had a greater chance for upward mobility to the status of freedmen. A newly-freed Missouri slave could play off the skills he or she learned in bondage and eventually get jobs as wagoners, blacksmiths, carpenters, house servants, cooks, waiters, draymen, stonemasons, watchmen, drivers, painters, gardeners, hostelers, stable keepers, merchants, chambermaids, laundresses, or seamstresses. And the authors note that while Missouri was home to a little more than 7 percent of the nation's free blacks, the state can be proud to have had within its borders the likes of many illustrious freedmen like John Berry Meachum, who, in the most ingenious of schemes, circumvented the legislation of 1847 which made it illegal to teach blacks to read and write. Meachum's craftiness looms even more remarkably when his roots are traced.

The nation's only two black U. S. Senators to precede Massachusetts Senator Brooke's 1966 election were freedmen who called Missouri home before they took their offices in Washington. The black explorer who founded Chicago eventually settled in Missouri's St. Charles County. And Missouri's freedmen who were too restless to settle down can be credited with spearheading much of the nation's exploration of and expansion into Colorado, Oregon, Washington, and other points west.

It may be hard for those of limited exposure to the nation's black history to imagine that there existed in Missouri, specifically in St. Louis, a "colored aristocracy" while slaves were still being held. One wealthy St. Louis freedman of the 1850s, a cattle dealer, had assets of $300,000—a healthy fortune even by today's standards. Despite the snobbishness of this elite circle of freedmen, and despite the circumscribed lives imposed on them by one Missouri law after another, they proved that enterprise and industriousness could neither be predicted nor subjugated because of racial heritage.

From the struggles which served as a prelude to the Civil War, through all of the war efforts which tested the nation's mettle—the Union against the Confederacy and the Union against world powers—Missouri's blacks carried themselves with a boldness, valor, and pride which belied their existing or past state of bondage. It is an incredible attestation to the desire of blacks to be a part of this country's fiber that they were able to fight for certain principles which did not reflect their own condition. Missouri's blacks, and blacks throughout the divided nation, fought as if the Union were truly theirs. They fought valiantly even though President Lincoln dragged his feet for two years of Civil War fighting before officially giving blacks the right to die on the battlefield. Records show that 8,400 Missouri blacks were recruited in 1864 to fight for the Union in poorly armed, segregated units for less pay than their white counterparts. In December of 1863, Missouri's 65th U. S. Colored Infantry was sent into battle without shoes, hats, uniforms, or food. More than a hundred soldiers in the 65th died in the two months which followed. Some black units were not paid until ten years after the Civil War ended! Despite the oppressive conditions under which the black soldier fought, Missouri ranked fifth among all states in the number of black troops called upon to put down the Confederacy.

The end of the Civil War found slaves in Missouri and throughout the country assured that a better day was coming. But as the newly freed slaves quickly found out, freedom and all its blessings would not bo handed to them on a silver platter.

As a result of a Missouri state convention in 1865, Missouri's slaves were actually given their freedom before the Thirteenth Amendment was passed. But violent pro-slavery elements lived on after the institution was officially declared dead in Missouri. Lynch mobs thwarted the efforts of Missouri's freedmen to be really free—especially in Boone, Howard, Randolph, and Callaway Counties. But with the aid of dedicated individuals and agencies, the state's freedmen were led in a determined march in the general direction of freedom and equality.

Missouri's blacks were intent on getting the civil rights they were due. One hundred years ago a delegation of Missouri blacks went to Washington to make their demands of the president. Black leaders met with Missouri's governor to make similar demands in 1881. A state convention of blacks was called in 1882. The state's blacks found that as many roadblocks to freedom could be thrown up by the Missouri Supreme Court and the U. S. Supreme Court as had been established by the slavemaster and the overseer. In fact, the courts seemed to take the place of the masters whose slaves were taken away from them by law. Blacks found that their pleas to the holders of the keys to equality were feeble persuasion. And as more and more black Missourians moved to the great urban centers of St. Louis and Kansas City, even the ballot turned out to be ineffective ammunition. In fact, the very thought by white racists that the black vote could become a formidable entity with which to reckon caused even more violence to Missouri blacks than against blacks in many other southern states. Fifty-one Missouri blacks were lynched in the thirty years which followed 1889. Perhaps there were many more lynchings which were not reported to or by authorities. To further compound the black struggle in Missouri, the problems caused by urbanization were monumental. Crime, hunger, and disease spread like wildfire through black ghettos and threatened alternately to wipe out the state's entire black population—the population which had survived bondage and oppression. The black death rate actually exceeded the black birth rate for years in some turn-of-the-century black ghettos.

Yet in defiance of the odds, Missouri blacks seemed to rise Phoenix-like from their ashes. They forged a sound but segregated educational system for blacks before the U. S. Supreme Court finally erased the "separate but equal" premise. Missouri blacks showed enterprise and a firm grasp of the tenets of capitalism early in their tenure in the state. Their inventiveness diminished back-breaking labor and bolstered the state's and the nation's economics. They learned, mastered, and created prolifically inside all the art forms. Missouri blacks even rose above their hardships to take center stage in teaching the nation to sing the blues, dance to Missouri-invented ragtime, and get lost in the moods of something that came to be known as jazz. And Missouri's blacks have made effective waves in the mainstream of the state's and the nation's political activity.

It is a matter of historical record that Missouri's black people have joined blacks in all the other states in marching through wars, blatant and latent discrimination, legal obstacles and sheer hatred in the pursuit of the same elusive dreams their ancestors pursued two hundred years ago. Perhaps some day that dream will be a reality. It is my firm belief that this book will contribute to the realization of that dream. It will, indeed, be a contributing factor as it educates those who are ignorant of the rich contributions of blacks to the state of Missouri and to the nation. This volume will make a great contribution as it swells pride within the chests of its black readers. It will give white readers a better understanding of the plight and problems blacks have experienced. This work will help to make the dream a reality as it corrects the gross errors and fills in the gaping holes so evident in traditional American history books. But *Missouri's Black Heritage* will have served a monumental purpose if it does no more than whet the appetite for an increased knowledge of the contributions of blacks in Missouri and in America.

Julius K. Hunter

The Black Experience in Missouri: A Personal View

Lorenzo J. Greene

I arrived in Jefferson City for the first time on a hot, sultry evening in September 1933. I had just completed an overnight trip from New York City to accept a position teaching history at Lincoln University. As I lugged my bags off the train, I had one overriding desire: to reach the university as quickly as possible. Fortunately, several taxis were parked near the station. I hailed one. The first white driver ignored me. The next let me have it straight: "We don't haul niggers. Get that 'nigger' cab over there." Stifling my anger, I took my bags to where two taxis, driven by blacks, were parked.

Enroute to the university, we passed through a slum area which the cab driver called "The Foot." The school stood atop a hill covered with beautiful trees, shrubbery, and flowers. It was a lovely sight. I was met by a French professor who was acting as caretaker while the president was out of town. He took me to Foster Hall, a freshman dorm, and gave me a room. I quickly showered, changed clothes, and sallied forth to my first meal in Jefferson City.

Across the street from the campus stood a small restaurant. As I approached it, my heart sank. A nauseating smell of rancid grease overwhelmed the fragrance of nearby honeysuckles. Worse, even before I crossed the street, the sight and sound of swarms of bugs and flies, covering and striking against the screen door of the restaurant, literally turned my stomach. I put on a bold face, flailed away at the insects, and quickly entered. The room was dingy and dirty. The proprietor, perspiring and swatting at the winged insects that seemed intent on taking over the place, offered me a seat. Knowing that it would be impossible for me to eat there, I ordered something not included on the menu. "Sorry," the waitress said unsmilingly, "but we are out of that." "Is there another restaurant nearby?" I asked. "Yes, there is one in the hotel down the street but it is closed now," the owner answered. I then inquired whether there was a drugstore open. "Four blocks down the street," the man replied.

The drugstore had a lunch counter. It was now nearly ten o'clock and I was hungry. I sat down at the counter. A young man asked me what I wanted. "A hamburger and a vanilla malted milk," I said. "I'm sorry," he replied, "but we don't serve colored here." I felt both angry and embarrassed, particularly since several white customers were intently watching me with smirks on their faces. Ignoring them, I asked the clerk whether he had vanilla ice cream. He replied that he did. "You can sell a colored person a pint of ice cream, can't you?" I asked sarcastically. "Yes," he answered. "Well, give me a pint of vanilla, and you *do* have *wooden* spoons?" Again an affirmative reply. "Then please put two of them in the bag with the ice cream!" He did so. I left the store, carrying my "supper" with me. Lonely and angry, I retraced my steps to the university. It was my first experience with racism in Jefferson City.

As I ate the ice cream in my dorm room, I looked out of the window. I was unaccustomed to the treatment I had just received. My hunger had left me. I was hurt and sad. All I could do was cry. Disillusioned and dejected, I decided that upon receiving my first paycheck, I would return to New York where the National Urban League had a housing job awaiting me, contingent upon a grant from Washington.

But events of the next few days changed my mind. The president, administrators, faculty members, and students began arriving, and the academic wheels started to turn. When classes began, I realized that my services were needed here. Lincoln had an excellent faculty, drawn from such prestigious universities as Harvard, Columbia, Chicago, Boston, New York, Pittsburgh, Cornell, and others. A group of us planned to make Lincoln an academic replica of Amherst. Student enrollment ranged between 300 and 350. We had the pick of black students from Missouri, Arkansas, Oklahoma, and other nearby states. Others came from as far away as California and Massachusetts. Many had excellent potential, but had been victimized by inferior, segregated schools. Soon, under a group of dedicated teachers, Lincoln was turning out students, many of whom enrolled for higher degrees in the best universities in the nation. Others entered the professions, especially as teachers. I had found my life's work and loved it.

I was also determined to help change the economic and social climate of Missouri—to break down segregation and discrimination. Over the years I aligned myself with various groups: the Missouri Association for Social Welfare, the Missouri Council of Churches, the Urban League, the NAACP, the Missouri Council of Labor, the League of Women Voters, liberal faculty members and students from various colleges and universities—Jews, Gentiles, professional workers and laymen—all united together in a crusade for social justice.

There were two struggles that have remained especially dear to me. One was the sharecroppers' protest in southeast Missouri. On January 1, 1939, white and black sharecroppers and tenant farmers of Butler, Pemiscot, Dunklin, and New Madrid counties were evicted by their landlords. On January 10, 1939, as a means of bringing their miserable plight before the world, they moved with their pitiable belongings on Highways 60 and 61. There, in rain, sleet, cold and snow, unable to obtain aid from local, state or federal authorities, the croppers eked out a precarious existence for months.

The striking farm workers demanded the abolition of the sharecropping and tenant farm system, the individual ownership of land, the organization of all farm workers, and wages of fifteen cents an hour for a ten-hour day and twenty cents an hour for all overtime. In addition, they wanted landlords to grant them the privilege of raising pigs and chickens; to furnish them with a milk cow, free pasture, a garden plot, and the use of a team to haul firewood; and to give them the right to raise corn and cotton on a fifty-fifty basis. Finally, they demanded teams or trucks to get their produce to market. When the landlords refused these demands, the sharecroppers walked off or were evicted from the plantations.

In April, I spoke to students and teachers at the Negro high school in Charleston and spent the weekend among the sharecroppers. What I saw shocked me: little children, their bellies swollen from lack of food; men, women, and children barefoot in the slush and snow; girls and women scantily clothed, wearing anything to keep warm; shelters made of cardboard, tin, pieces of wood, twigs, anything to protect them from the elements; girls and women cooking out-of-doors with snow and sleet falling into their kettles; and a small church providing temporary housing for nearly one hundred people.

On returning to Lincoln, I told my class in American history about the condition of the sharecroppers. I described their suffering, the sickness, the starving children and their pitiable attempts to maintain their dignity and strength in the face of almost impossible odds. I asked, "How many of you are from Southeast Missouri?" About ten of my thirty-five students raised their hands. "How many of you have heard about the sharecroppers' demonstrations?" Fewer hands were raised. Student interest increased and the discussion consumed the entire class period. One student inquired, "Did the sharecroppers ask what we thought of their condition?" I replied, "Nothing, you are too busy preparing for your spring prom."

Unknown to myself, I had dropped a bomb. Following my second class, while sitting in my office, a knock sounded on the door. Opening it, three young women entered. One of them began: "Mr. Greene, we heard what you said about the sharecroppers and we felt ashamed. So, we called an emergency meeting of the AKA sorority. And we want to ask you a question. Would it be OK if we let our prom go and gave the money to the sharecroppers? We have three hundred dollars."

They left, and soon representatives of the Deltas came in offering the same sacrifice. Before I left for lunch, the president of the Student Council came to tell me that her organization had pledged eighty dollars to aid the sharecroppers. The sororities, particularly the AKA's and Deltas, gave, solicited, bought, and mended clothing. Other students and faculty members did the same. Money intended for proms went for clothing, food, cartons of baby food, sugar, cod liver oil, cereal, disinfectants, soap, and the like. Shoes, rubbers, and hats added to the collection. About three hundred dollars in cash was left over.

When all was ready we had amassed nearly a truck full of clothing, shoes, food, medicine, and other necessities. Off we went, the president allowing three young women who had led the campaign to accompany me to Southeast Missouri. The sharecroppers welcomed us with profuse expressions of thanks. The girls washed and fed the babies and children, and helped the women with their chores.

We made several more trips to Southeast Missouri. I wrote newspaper and magazine articles and letters to individuals, imploring them to aid the sharecroppers and displaced tenant farmers in any way possible. From various parts of the country came contributions of clothing, small donations of money, and letters, inquiring in what way they could help these unfortunate people.

In 1940, we bought land for the sharecroppers, built homes, and helped settle some near Poplar Bluff. Finally, the Farm Security Administration came to the rescue, and aided in settling the sharecroppers in homes which they could buy on easy payments. When they could not keep up the payments, we established a volunteer corporation, guaranteed their payments, and set up a store at Lilbourn. There the croppers could obtain food, clothing, and other items donated by involved persons for a pittance or even obtain things, if penniless, free of charge. The project is still in operation at Lilbourn.

The second cause that has remained particularly dear to me was the setting up of the State Human Rights Commission. For several years, this had been high on the priorities of the Missouri Association for Social Welfare and its affiliated organizations. The Missouri Association, labor and church groups, professionals, and laymen decided to utilize a bipartisan, biracial strategy that included the support of members of both House and Senate. A Civil Rights bill was introduced in both Houses simultaneously.

A key factor was the gubernatorial campaign of 1956. James A. Blair, a liberal Democrat, was running for governor as an independent. His support would be crucial to setting up a state Commission on Human Rights. For the statewide support which our groups promised him, he pledged his word to see that we got our wish. Blair won the election. Only after a furious struggle in the legislature, in which Blair personally intervened, was the bill passed. The purpose of the bill was to eliminate segregation and discrimination in Missouri. Blair later signed it into law, and we had our first Human Rights Commission.

How can we assess the results of our efforts over the years? Spurred by the civil rights movement of the late fifties, sixties, and early seventies, places of public accommodation were opened to all persons. Hotels, motels, restaurants, theaters, public schools, and colleges all willingly or unwillingly desegregated. Black and white children studied together. Appeals to state courts and the liberalism of the United States Supreme Court under Chief Justice Earl Warren witnessed the opening of state, municipal, and private employment, and the upgrading of blacks in occupations. Black history gave both blacks and whites a truer picture of American civilization. In general, we moved closer to the egalitarian society envisaged in the immortal Declaration of Independence. This is enhanced now by the larger number of blacks elected or appointed to public offices.

And what of tomorrow? The picture is not as bright as it could be. Black employment, especially among youth, is at an all-time low; the social climate of the sixties and early seventies has given way to a more conservative and even reactionary one; hate groups, like the KKK and Neo-Nazis, brazenly attempt to turn the clock back by preaching the outworn gospel of a "white-people's country." Desegregation of schools is giving way to resegregation in the inner cities as whites flee increasingly to the suburbs. Unemployed blacks turn more and more to crime and drugs. Black study courses in colleges and universities find their budgets cut as these institutions seek to accomplish more with less financial backing. Schoolchildren are being short-changed by insufficient school funding, teachers' strikes, and discipline problems. In short, the struggle for human rights, which held such bright prospects less than a decade ago, is now a fragmented movement, whose consequences for the future are impossible to predict.

What is needed is a return to the unified movement of the sixties when whites and blacks, Jews and Gentiles, student groups, liberal political leaders, and an enlightened judiciary dedicated themselves to peaceful means for achieving equal rights for all people. We have made progress, yes! But we have a long way to go.

Roots:
Slavery Comes to Missouri

America was an exciting and awesome challenge to the Europeans. The North American continent was a vast new world more than twice the size of Europe. Who discovered America? The American Indians from Asia, blacks from Africa, or Norsemen from Europe? While the actual discoverers of America may forever remain a mystery to historians, Christopher Columbus is generally credited with paving the way for European colonization when he made his famous voyage in 1492. Generations of Spanish, English, and French explorers and settlers from all over the world followed. The people of the old world brought with them many different ideas, institutions, and ways of life. Each contributed in a unique way to the creation of a new country.

Slavery was not a new institution in America, or indeed, in the world. All peoples at one time have been enslaved. Slavery is as old as warfare, which means as old as the existence of people on this earth. The victors in battle usually killed or enslaved the vanquished. Slavery for financial gain emerged only after mankind developed agriculture.

The first slaves in America were Indians. Indian tribes living in the Missouri and Mississippi river valleys before the coming of Europeans often fought with one another. And just as in the ancient world, victors became masters and losers slaves. But the Indians of North America practiced a different type of slavery from their white successors. They did not sell or trade their slaves, at least not until they came in contact with the Europeans. Rather, they made their captives tribal members who were entitled to the rights and privileges conferred on other members of the group. In that regard, they engaged in a form of slavery that closely resembled what went on in Africa before the Europeans entered that continent.

Black slavery was introduced into America by the Spanish, English, and French. Slavery was no respecter of color, however. Red, white, and black peoples alike were sold into bondage because of the pressing need for labor. Black slaves were to play an invaluable role in the history of America and Missouri. They brought with them a rich heritage and played a vital part in the shaping of a new nation. In the pages which follow we will trace the trials and triumphs, the sorrows and joys, the achievements and contributions of the black heritage in Missouri.

The French, the Spanish, and Slavery

The French Explorers. The French first settled the area which today is eastern Canada. In the 1670s and 1680s, they ventured westward to the great lakes and then southward down the Mississippi toward its mouth in the Gulf of Mexico, naming the valley west of the river "Louisiana" after their king, Louis XIV. The first Frenchmen were trappers and fur traders who formed trading posts along the river routes.

The arrival of French explorers and traders radically changed slavery among the Indians. The French wanted to buy Indian slaves, providing tribes such as the Osage and Missouri with guns and ammunition in return for captives. Once one tribe had acquired weapons, other groups felt compelled to do the same. Consequently, rather than a *by-product* of conflict, slavery became its *cause*. The only way to avoid becoming enslaved was to be stronger than an enemy tribe. One way to do that was to capture slaves and barter them for weapons. The rise of slave-trading for gain had begun.

Eventually the French government decided to develop upper Louisiana (the area including present-day Missouri and Arkansas). French officials entrusted the job to a corporation known as the Company of the West. The Company set up headquarters on the Illinois side of the Mississippi River. Soon after, it sent Marc Antoine de la Leere des Ursins across the river in search of potential mining sites.

Missouri's First Blacks. The first black slaves to enter what would later

EARLY FRENCH SETTLEMENTS

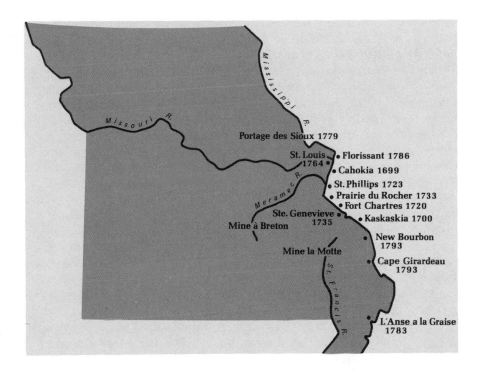

Portage des Sioux 1779

St. Louis 1764

Florissant 1786

Cahokia 1699

St. Phillips 1723

Prairie du Rocher 1733

Fort Chartres 1720

Kaskaskia 1700

Ste. Genevieve 1735

Mine à Breton

New Bourbon 1793

Mine la Motte

Cape Girardeau 1793

L'Anse a la Graise 1783

be Missouri probably arrived in 1719, unwilling participants in the new French mining venture. Des Ursins brought five blacks with him, and although he failed to find the silver mines he sought, he did discover several rich lead deposits. In 1720, Phillippe François Renault was sent from France to direct lead-mining operations. He may have brought with him as many as 500 black slaves from the French island of Haiti. These were the first permanent black residents of Missouri. The Company of the West contracted to supply Renault with twenty-five additional blacks annually. By 1725, Renault's mines were yielding fifteen hundred pounds of lead a day.

Throughout the early years of the eighteenth century, blacks rapidly replaced Indian slaves. Why the change? One reason was that the continued enslavement of Indians by whites threatened to destroy peaceful commercial relations between the Europeans and their Indian neighbors. Whites were greatly outnumbered by Indians, but they found security in the fact that tribes often fought with each other. The issue of slavery threatened to provide the Indians with a common cause to unite against the Europeans. Furthermore, the Indian was at home in the Mississippi and Missouri river valleys. He could escape his white owner, flee back to his village, and disappear into the tribe unnoticed by the master. Whites who enslaved Indians were taking a risk. Thrifty Frenchmen feared seeing slaves, who had cost them expensive guns, run off before they could realize a return on their investment. The black slave, on the other hand, was thousands of miles from home. He was not familiar with the terrain, and his black skin was immediately noticeable anywhere in the New World. He was, the Frenchmen reasoned, the answer to their labor problems. By the time St. Louis was founded in 1764, black slavery had become a widely accepted and crucially important mainstay of the French-American economy.

Spanish Rule. The American colonies could not be developed peacefully by the Europeans because the major European states were frequently at war with each other. During the seventeenth and eighteenth centuries, Spain and France each fought England, and the colonies were both pawns in the struggle and prizes for the victors. The end of the French and Indian War, or Seven Years' War (1756-63), revealed just how high the stakes were. France went down to defeat at the hands of the English. Spain had entered the war in 1762 on the side of the French to prevent an English victory, but the allies were defeated by the British on land and sea. To pay Spain for her losses, France transferred to the Spanish all of the Louisiana Territory.

Slaves were used quite differently under Spanish rule. While the French had employed blacks primarily in the mining industry, Spain used them mainly to supply the mother country with agricultural goods. In 1777, Governor Bernardo de Galvez ordered Lieutenant Governor Francisco Cruzat to encourage the production of hemp and flax in upper Louisiana. Cruzat replied that this was impossible without black slaves and that since most of the settlers were poor, the slaves would have to be sold on credit. Galvez assured Cruzat there would be no problem, since the king of France had already contracted to supply the settlers with slaves.

The United States

A New Nation Created. Meanwhile, momentous changes were taking place east of the Mississippi River. England had long controlled the thirteen colonies along the Atlantic Coast. England's victory in the French and Indian War had added to her possessions Canada and all

Slave auction. *(State Historical Society of Missouri)*

the territory in America between the Allegheny Mountains and the Mississippi River. The tremendous expanse of new territory caused Britain to revise her colonial policies by taxing her colonies to help pay her war debts. Americans reacted with hostility to the change in their relationship with the mother country. They resorted to open and armed rebellion in 1775, claimed freedom from England in 1776 in the Declaration of Independence, and then after eight years of warfare won their independence. The thirteen united colonies became the United States of America.

Slavery was an important source of disagreement in the vast new American nation which stretched from the Atlantic to the Mississippi. In fact, it came near wrecking the Constitutional Convention which met at Philadelphia in 1787 to draw up a stronger instrument of government for the United States. Southern states wanted the slaves counted as residents of the states in which they lived for purposes of political representation, but did not want the slaves to be counted when it came to levying taxes. Northerners took the opposite position. They wanted slaves counted for taxation, but not representation. Both sections finally agreed to the famous "three-fifths compromise." Slaves would be counted as three-fifths of a person both for purposes of representation and taxation. Thus the slaves became victims of their skin color. In addition, slavery would be forbidden in the territory north of the Ohio River (the present states of Wisconsin, Illinois, Michigan, Ohio, and Indiana). One of the immediate effects of this Northwest Ordinance, as it was known, was that many American slaveowners living east of the Mississippi River and north of the Ohio River crossed into Spanish-controlled Missouri territory to avoid losing their slaves.

The Vital Mississippi River. The Mississippi was more than a barrier separating America from the Spanish colonial possessions. It was the major means by which American farmers in the Mississippi valley could float their produce downstream to the ocean port of New Orleans. From New Orleans, the goods could be shipped to markets in England and Europe. The problem was that Spain controlled New Orleans and thus the United States had to negotiate with Spain. The new nation asked for permission to deposit goods at New Orleans until they could be loaded on ships carrying them across the ocean. That arrangement was written into the Treaty of San Lorenzo in 1795.

The Louisiana Purchase

The French Revolution and Napoleon. In 1789 a violent revolution broke out in France, in part inspired by the example of the American Revolution. As the French people struggled with the difficult task of shaping a new government and claiming personal liberties in their Declaration of the Rights of Man, all of Europe became involved—and with the European states, all their colonies in America. After Napoleon took control of the French government in 1799, he quickly invaded and conquered Spain in 1800. He demanded that Spain give him all of the Louisiana Territory. Napoleon hoped to make the French West Indian island of Haiti his base for building an empire in the Americas. Napoleon's army was to take control of New Orleans in 1803.

The American president, Thomas Jefferson, was well aware of the danger posed by a French-controlled New Orleans. France was the world's strongest military power at the time. Holding New Orleans, it could prevent American farmers from shipping their produce down the Ohio and Mississippi rivers to the markets of Europe. President Jefferson, although disliking England, decided he would ally America with England to ensure American farmers the right of deposit at the port of New Orleans.

But the blacks in Haiti had been inspired by the Declaration of Independence and the Declaration of the Rights of Man, and the same freedom promised the French. Haiti in 1789 had a black population of 500,000 slaves. All were cruelly exploited by a few thousand whites,

THE LOUISIANA TERRITORY

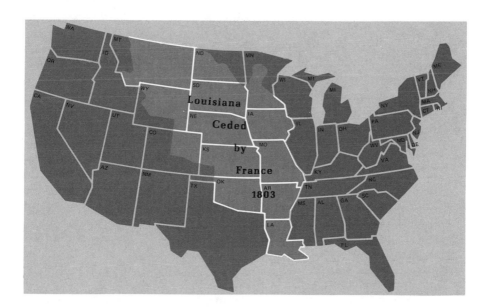

mostly French planters and government officials. The slaves rebelled against their white masters in 1791 and for more than a decade they defeated French, Spanish, and British armies sent to subdue them. They were led by three great black generals: Toussaint L'Ouverture, Jean Jacques Dessalines, and Henri Christophe. Napoleon lost forty thousand of his best troops to the slaves who declared their independence in 1803. The rebellion shattered Napoleon's dream of a great empire in America dominated by France. Black opposition had made this impossible. Indeed, it made possible the expansion of the United States to the Pacific.

France Sells Louisiana. While the revolution of the black slaves was raging in Haiti, President Jefferson was trying to buy New Orleans from Napoleon. Eager to secure that ocean port as a trade depot for American goods, he sent James Monroe and Robert Livingstone to France in the hope that Napoleon would sell the southern city and the land to the east of it for ten million dollars. By the time the Americans arrived, Napoleon had already lost Haiti and he feared that the English fleet would take over New Orleans. Consequently, he astounded the American envoys by asking them, "What would you give for all of Louisiana?" Although shocked by Napoleon's willingness to part with the entire territory, the American envoys quickly regained their composure and, after some haggling, bought all the land between the Mississippi River and the Rocky Mountains for fifteen million dollars. The American nation's size more than doubled overnight. The region out of which Missouri was carved came under the United States flag in large part because of the courageous struggle of the Haitian blacks for their freedom.

The Missouri Territory

The Growth of Missouri. America's purchase of Louisiana in 1803 was followed by a dramatic increase in the population of that territory. As the number of settlers moving into the new land increased, so did the number of slaves they brought with them to conquer the frontier. At the time of the Louisiana Purchase there were 10,340 persons living in Missouri. Blacks numbered 1,320, or nearly 13 percent of the total population. By 1810 Missouri's population had grown to 20,845, or an increase of more than 101 percent. During that same period the black population grew to 3,618.

Missouri attracted settlers for many reasons. Most importantly, its soil was quite rich, especially in the Missouri River bottoms. Thus it held out the promise for profitable agricultural production. When Missouri became a state in 1821, approximately three-fourths of its citizens were engaged in farming. The fact that Missouri allowed slavery also made it attractive.

Slavery and the Black Codes. The majority of Missouri's slaves were located in the Mississippi and Missouri river valleys. St. Louis, of course, led the way. The commander of the Missouri Territory, Captain Ames Stoddard, reported that there were 667 slaves in the District of St. Louis in 1804. That number increased to 740 for St. Louis County by 1810. Other areas with high concentrations of slaves in those early days of the territory included St. Charles, Ste. Genevieve, and Cape Girardeau.

Even before the Louisiana Purchase, the number of slaves was large enough to make white settlers afraid of slave uprisings. The French and Spanish had enacted "Black Codes," making it illegal for slaves to leave their owner's property without his permission, to carry guns, to strike their masters, or to own property. Even these rigid rules could not stifle completely the black slave's desire to be free. In 1781, for example, Lt. Gov. Francisco Cruzat expressed concern about the

rowdy and rebellious slaves of St. Louis and called for a stricter enforcement of the Black Codes.

The slaveowners of the new Missouri Territory had even more
reason to be fearful. The rebellion of Toussaint L'Ouverture and his
followers in Haiti had struck fear in the hearts of southern slaveowners.
Within the United States there had been an unsuccessful revolt in 1800
by Gabriel Prosser, who had planned to lead a band of over one thousand slaves on Richmond, Virginia. Therefore, one of the first things
the new territorial government of Missouri did was to enact a new
series of Black or Slave Codes, patterned closely after those of Virginia.
Many Missourians had migrated from Virginia and carried with them
memories of Prosser and of the code that Virginians had enacted to
forestall another revolt.

The code of 1804 in Missouri made no distinction between slaves
and other property. Slaves could not testify in court against whites
and they could not leave their owner's farm or plantation without his
permission. Likewise, they could not own or carry guns. The code
also attempted to define exactly who was a black person. It declared
that "any person who shall have one-fourth part or more of negro
blood" was to be considered a black person and bound to obey the
Black Codes. Practically speaking, that meant that if a person had
three white grandparents and one black grandparent, he or she would
still be considered to be black.

The Need for Slaves Increases. The decade of the 1810s saw Missouri's
population grow even more rapidly than before. Several factors contributed to this growth. The ending of the War of 1812 and the Napo-
leonic Wars in 1815 made migration from the old world easier. Likewise, the Industrial Revolution played a crucial role in making the
Western territory attractive. Developments in the cotton industry
were particularly important to this process. The power loom, an automatic machine used to weave yarn, replaced hand-operated equipment
in the early nineteenth century. This advancement, combined with
Eli Whitney's invention of the cotton gin, greatly increased the demand for cotton in America. In 1790 approximately 750,000 pounds of
cotton were produced. Seventy years later cotton production in
America reached more than two billion pounds.

With such an increase in the demand for cotton, producers of
that commodity quite naturally looked for land on which they could
expand their operations. Many people believed that the Louisiana
Territory, and, in particular, Missouri, would provide the added land
needed to expand cotton production. Ultimately, some cotton was
produced in Missouri, particularly in the southern part, but the state

Slave bill of sale. *(State Historical Society of Missouri)*

never became a large producer because of its relatively short growing season. Farming was intensive, however, and the use of slave labor increased its profitability.

Slavery and Statehood

In no territory would the issue of slavery and the seeking of statehood be more closely intertwined than in Missouri. Although Missourians could not have anticipated it at the time, their request to be admitted to the United States would result in one of the most important political battles the country has ever known. By 1820, the Missouri Territory claimed unofficially to have 56,016 white residents and 10,222 slaves. Citizens began clamoring for statehood. The controversy centered around the status of blacks in Missouri. Should they be slave or free? The debate over that question was a rehearsal for the great crisis that eventually split the country into civil war in 1861.

The Battle in Congress. The dilemma created by Missouri's application for statehood was a difficult one to resolve. The population of the North was growing faster than that of the South. Representation in the United States House of Representatives was based on population. The populous northern, nonslaveholding states soon outnumbered the representatives of the southern slavocracy. The southerners feared that opponents of slavery, known as antislaveryites, would win a congressional fight to restrict or even eliminate slavery.

The slave states had only one chance of avoiding that outcome. Since a bill could not become law unless it passed through both houses of Congress, the South would concentrate on winning its battle in the Senate. Representation in that body was allocated on the basis of statehood, with each state, regardless of its size, being entitled to two senators. If the South could maintain a balance of slave states equal in number to free states, it could thwart attempts at abolishing slavery.

That was much easier said than done, however. In March 1818, Missouri's territorial representative, John Scott, petitioned Congress for Missouri's admission to the Union. There were eleven free and ten slave states. Alabama soon balanced the situation, however, by becoming the eleventh slave state.

What would now happen with Missouri's petition? To admit her as a slave state would break the recently achieved Senate balance in favor of the South. To do otherwise would favor the free states. Not to admit her at all would be contrary to the Constitution, which provided that when a territory had a population equal to that of the least populous state it could ask Congress for admission to the Union. Once permission was given, the territory could draw up a Constitution. The next step, after approval of the Constitution, was statehood.

Missouri applied for admission into the Union as a slave state. On February 13, 1819, Congressman James Tallmadge of New York proposed that Missouri come into the Union as a slave state but that no more slaves be allowed to enter the territory. He also proposed that the slaves already there be set free whenever they reached the age of twenty-five. Tallmadge's bill barely passed in· the House. A combination of southerners and northern proslavery senators defeated it in the Senate.

The Missouri Compromise. The issue was raised again in the next session of Congress. By that time, the whole nation was astir with the arguments of pro and antislaveryites. It seemed as if the entire nation was holding its breath, waiting to see if and how the controversy would be resolved. Astute observers of the controversy surrounding Missouri's attempt to become a state could see that the fight over slavery had only begun and that it would continue to inspire fierce hatred on both sides. To the aged Thomas Jefferson the Missouri question was as frightening as the sound of a "firebell in the night."

After a furious struggle, Missouri entered as a slave state and northeastern Massachusetts, now known as Maine, entered as a free state. The balance between the number of slave and free states in the Senate was preserved. While Missouri was allowed to come into the

Fugitive slave fleeing on foot. *(State Historical Society of Missouri)*

Union as a slave state, all the land north of 36°30′ not located within the boundaries of Missouri was to be forever free.

Missouri as a Slave State. While the debate over whether or not to admit slavery had been raging in the United States Congress, a similar struggle was carried on in Missouri. On March 6, 1820, Congress had authorized the people of the territory to come together and write a constitution for their new state. Proslaveryites dominated the convention. When word was brought that Congress was willing to allow slavery to exist in Missouri, the delegates rejoiced. One man even went so far as to try to persuade his fellow Missourians that blacks themselves were exceedingly happy over this bit of news. After all, he argued, the Missouri Compromise meant that blacks would not have to live "in the uncomfortable surroundings of states such as Virginia, Kentucky, and Tennessee; they could be brought to the infinitely more pleasant confines of Missouri!"

The Missouri question having finally been resolved, President James Monroe proclaimed Missouri to be the twenty-fourth state of the Union on August 10, 1821. As a state, Missouri embarked upon a plan of expansion rivaled by few other territories in pre-Civil War America. The black presence had already been strongly felt in Missouri. The complexities of life that accompanied statehood would only cause black and white lives to become more intertwined.

SUGGESTED READINGS

The best general work on the origins of Missouri is William E. Foley's book in the Missouri sesquicentennial edition of *A History of Missouri*, I, *1673-1820* (Columbia, 1971). Russell Magnaghi's essay "The Role of Indian Slavery in Colonial St. Louis," *Bulletin* [Missouri Historical Society], XXXI (July 1975), pages 264-272, reveals much about early Indian slavery in the region.

The classic work on black slavery in the Missouri Territory remains Harrison A. Trexler, *Slavery in Missouri 1804-1865* (Baltimore, 1914). It should be supplemented by the following articles: Lloyd A. Hunter, "Slavery in St. Louis 1804-1860," *Bulletin* [Missouri Historical Society], XXX (July 1974), pages 233-265; Emil Oberholzer, "The Legal Aspects of Slavery in Missouri," *Bulletin* [Missouri Historical Society], VI [in three parts] (January 1950), pages 139-161, (April 1950), pages 333-351, and (July 1950), pages 540-545; and Arvarh E. Strickland, "Aspects of Slavery in Missouri, 1821," *Missouri Historical Review*, LXV (July 1971), pages 505-526.

The standard work on the Missouri Compromise is Glover Moore, *The Missouri Controversy, 1819 1821* (Lexington, Kentucky, 1953).

2

From Sunup to Sundown:
The Life of the Slave

Slavery was, above all else, an economic institution. Slavemasters were interested in getting as much work out of their slaves as they could for as long as possible. The life of the slave was determined largely by this fact. Contrary to what some historians once supposed, slavery remained a profitable and viable institution right down to the Civil War. Indeed, in some regions, such as Callaway County, Missouri, slavery was the most important factor in the maintenance of the economy.

Slavery in Missouri

The Versatility of Missouri Slaves. Missouri slaves had a wider range of skills and occupations than slaves in the deep South, because of the different type of farming in Missouri. In areas of the deep South such as Georgia and Mississippi, cotton was king, the primary crop, and most slaves did the same kind of work on huge plantations. Missouri's land was abundant and fertile, but the colder weather meant a shorter growing season and did not permit the growth of cotton in large quantities. So Missouri farmers—and the slaves they used—practiced mixed farming. They produced hemp, tobacco, wheat, oats, hay, corn, and other

PERCENTAGE OF SLAVES BY COUNTY, 1860

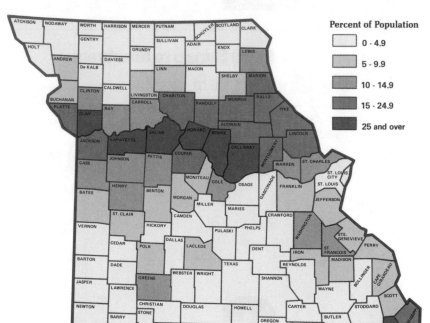

feed grains. Missouri also became well known for its fine cattle, sheep, horses, and pigs. Consequently the Missouri slave became a many-talented worker.

The majority of Missouri's slaves worked as field hands on farms, but there were many other occupations as well. They were also employed as valets, butlers, handy-men, carpenters, common laborers, maids, nurses, and cooks. Many Missouri masters hired their slaves out when they were not using them. That allowed the slaveowner to receive payment for the services of his slave, instead of allowing the slave to be idle. It also meant that the person hiring the slave had to take care of his room and board. That further reduced the master's expenses. Slaves often found themselves being hired out to work in mines, such as the Maramec Iron Works, for one hundred dollars a year. When railroads began moving through Missouri, black slaves were called upon to serve at the rate of twenty dollars a month. Brick-yards paid a similar sum for the slave's services. Many slaves were hired out to the owners of river boats. They worked as deck hands, cabin boys, or stevedores for approximately fifteen dollars a month. These wages were usually less than those paid whites for similar work.

Missouri's Slave Population. Missouri's population grew rapidly during the decades after she became a state. People from the states of Kentucky, Tennessee, North Carolina, and Virginia, attracted by the virgin Missouri soil, poured into the state. Many of the settlers brought slaves, and those who did not carried with them the hope that they would one day become slaveowners.

The following figures offer some idea of the rapid growth of slavery in the state before the Civil War:

MISSOURI'S POPULATION, 1810-1860

Year	Total Population	Whites	Slaves	Free Blacks	Percent Slaves of Pop.
1810	20,845	17,227	3,011	607	14.5
1820	66,586	54,903	9,797	376	15.4
1830	140,455	115,364	25,091	569	17.8
1840	383,702	322,295	57,891	1,478	15.5
1850	682,044	592,004	87,422	2,618	12.8
1860	1,182,012	1,063,489	114,931	3,572	9.8

These figures reveal that the white population of Missouri increased fifty-seven fold between 1810 and 1860. The slave population increased almost thirty-five fold during the same period. In 1830 slaves represented 17.8 percent of the total Missouri population. By 1860 that percentage had dropped to about 9.8.

Although there were many slaves, there were few large slaveholding plantations in Missouri. Only thirty-six of Missouri's 113 counties had one thousand or more slaves. Of course, some slavemasters did own quite a number of blacks. Jabez F. Smith of Jackson County owned 165 blacks at one time. John W. Ragland of Cooper County owned seventy slaves. He was the largest slaveowner in that county. Daniel Ligon, the largest slaveowner in Lewis County, had twenty-six slaves. Most Missourians owned none, and for those who did, the average was four blacks per slaveholding family. When there were only one or two slaves, the master and his family often worked along with the blacks.

What areas of Missouri had most slaves? They were not equally dispersed throughout the state. By 1830 the largest number of them were in Boone, Pike, Randolph, Wayne, and New Madrid counties, where they worked on the fertile farmlands of river bottoms. Hemp was the main single crop they cultivated.

The Slaveowners' Attitudes

Superiority and Inferiority. What was it like to be a slave in Missouri? Even the best treated black slave stood in a servile position to all of white society. Missouri slavery, from the owners' point of view, was justified on economic, spiritual, and social grounds. Blacks were regarded as inferior. The master argued that he was doing them a favor by enslaving them. Slavemasters even went so far as to argue that blacks were grateful to whites for their enslavement!

Nobody expressed this idea better than United States Senator James Green of Lewis County. In 1849 he wrote that there were "Two distinct races, one vastly inferior to the other. . . ." The white race was obviously superior to the black race, he continued, and blacks were obligated to be subservient to whites in all things. That arrangement had "resulted to the black in immense good, an incalculable benefit, both moral and physical." According to Green, blacks were not only inferior to whites, but "happy inferiors." He went on to note that "Our Negro is a sleek, fat-sided fellow. He loves to eat and to laugh, and give him his bellyfull and he is as happy as a prince. Work is his element. Meat and bread and the banjo are his happiness." Present scholarship does not accept this description of the slave; it is a stereotype invented by slaveowners in response to attacks by abolitionists upon slavery.

Slavery was an inhuman institution. Slaves were supposed to be protected by law from excessively harsh treatment. Any person found guilty of cruel or inhuman treatment of slaves was to be fined or sent to jail. But slaveholders paid little or no attention to the law. For example, the spectacle of a female slave whose master left her hanging by her thumbs in St. Louis in 1839, and other similar forms of cruel treatment, were not uncommon.

The harsh system of slavery was able to exist only by forcing blacks to stand in awe of whites. Slavemasters, as a group, were willing to use whatever means they could to instill fear into slaves. They believed a fearful slave would also be an obedient slave. But fear was a double-edged sword. Slavemasters realized that their ill-treatment of slaves would inspire black resentment. Consequently, they sought an elaborate system of laws to protect themselves, their families, and their communities against any semblance of black resistance. They

Whipping a slave. *(State Historical Society of Missouri)*

tried to enlist the support of nonslaveholding whites. Through religion, philosophy, law, and social practice, they tried to convince the
lowliest white person that he was better than the most cultured and
intelligent black. Whites of all classes were encouraged to believe
that they could some day enhance their social status by becoming
slaveowners. But seven out of eight Missouri families would never
own slaves.

Slaves as Property. Missouri's slave codes illustrate the general attitude toward blacks during the antebellum period. Slaves were desig-

nated as personal property, to be taxed, bought and sold, just like any other property. They were advertised in newspapers along with other merchandise. In 1835 Joseph Hardeman of Cole County offered for sale "one Negro man, one Negro woman, and three children ages 10, 12, and 16." Hardeman noted that the "man is a good plowman, woman and children good field hands." Six years later an Osage County master offered for sale a black youth named Samuel for five hundred dollars. Likewise, in 1851 Edward Lewis and his wife listed a young black with animals and other miscellaneous "merchandise" they had for sale:

> One Negro boy named Tom aged about fourteen years, one Bay Mare aged three this spring, one yoke of steers aged three years this spring, three young cows, one yearling mule, sixty barrels of corn all for the sum of nine hundred and fifty-five dollars.

The Slaves' Way of Life

Food and Housing. As to the needs of the slave—food, clothing, shelter, care when sick—in most cases these items rested in the hands of the owners. Whether the slave had sufficient food has always been a highly debated question. One student of Cole County slavery says that blacks had an unbalanced diet of cornbread and potatoes. Another historian says that slaves occasionally had pork, beef, or mutton. Of course, a master might allow the slave a little time on Saturday or Sunday to grow a few vegetables. The enterprising slave might supplement his diet with 'possums, rabbits, squirrels, or fish.

Housing for slaves varied, but was generally inadequate. Sometimes where there were only one or two slaves, they might sleep in the master's house. Where several were owned, they generally lived in cabins. There they cooked, slept, and socialized if they were not too tired from the day's work. Slave housing gave them little privacy. Daniel Ligon of Lewis County had only two houses for ten slaves. Slave quarters were not spacious by any means. The quarters of one owner consisted of small log cabins about twelve to fourteen feet square, an area smaller than most modern-day bedrooms. They were usually uncomfortable—extremely hot in summer, cold in winter, poorly lighted, and unsanitary. Some idea of the crowded conditions of slave housing can be seen in Cole County. Slaves were herded into cramped quarters like cattle. At one point there were 987 slaves in the county sharing only 90 cabins, an average of nearly 11 slaves per cabin.

Clothing and Health Care. Clothing, like housing and food, depended upon the master. Some masters clothed their slaves better than others, but most looked for the cheapest way out. Materials used were largely tow cloth, white and striped linsey, and heavy brown jeans. An advertisement for a runaway slave often offered evidence as to how slaves might be clothed: a slave who ran away in 1835 carried with him "two cotton shirts, one pair of linen pants, one green blanket, a coat, one pair of brown pants, and an old fur coat."

A newspaper in 1847 stated that a master, R. C. Cordell of Jefferson City, clothed three slaves—Lydia for twenty-four dollars for two years, Mary Ann for fifteen dollars for two years, and Pennett for forty dollars for one year—a total of seventy-nine dollars. An old slave related that the Missouri bondsmen generally received two pairs of trousers, two shirts, and a hat in summer; a coat, a pair of trousers, and a pair of shoes were provided in winter.

Blacks who were suffering from physical illnesses were generally cared for by their fellow slaves. Sometimes a doctor might be procured by a master eager to protect his investment. Often doctors were not available, however, since the frontier did not lend itself to attracting medical practitioners any more than the rural community does today. The slave midwife generally delivered the children and frequently cared for the master's offspring.

Recreation and Religion. Although Missouri bondsmen were generally worked from sunup to sundown during the week, they were often allowed Saturday afternoons to themselves. During that time, they might manufacture small articles for sale, perform odd jobs, or tend to a small plot of land adjoining the slave quarters. They were usually allowed to keep the money they made from these ventures. Often they applied their profits to the purchase of their freedom from the master. At times they were allowed to sing, swim, and to hold dances in the evening. Occasionally they attended a circus.

Master and slave generally attended the same church. The structure of religious worship left no doubt in the slave's mind of his inferiority. Generally slaves were physically separated from their masters and other whites. They were put either in a loft above the rest of the congregation, or in a special section of pews at the rear of the meetinghouse. They often heard sermons in which white ministers counseled them to be obedient and submissive to their masters. Black communicants participated in the sacraments only after all the whites had partaken. Even in death the races were generally separated. There were almost always "white" and "colored" cemeteries in every area of the state occupied by blacks.

Marriage. The Missouri slave code forbade the marriage of slaves. Sometimes a man and woman just "took up" with each other. Other

CANDIDATES
IN BOONE COUNTY.
FOR THE SENATE.

William Jewell. | A. M. Robinson.

REPRESENTATIVES.

Sinclair Kirtley, | Austin A. King,
Thos. C. Maupin, | Jesse B. Dale,
John B. Gordon, | John Henderson.
Tyre Harris, | Lawrence Bass.

JUSTICES COUNTY COURT.

Michael Woods, | Edmund S. Feild,
Joseph W. Hickam, | William Lientz,
Overton Harris, | Jesse Hart.
James W. Daly, | James Gordon.

SHERIFF.

John Parker, | William S. Burch
George C. Dale, | James H. Hinkson

CORONER.

Jacob Bruner, | Henry L. Douglas
Constable Columbia Township.
William Lampton, | Peter Kerney.
James K. Wright, | Augustus Hart.

THE LAND OFFICE

AT FAYETTE, will be re-opened for business on TUESDAY the 8th of July, 1834, at 10 o'clock, A. M

URIEL SEBREE, *Receiver.*
HAMPTON L. BOON, *Register.*
June 24, 1834.   1 2w

TEN DOLLARS REWARD.

BROKE away from me, in the neighborhood of Troy, on Wednesday the 28th of May last, a fine Bay Horse, about fifteen hands and a half high, of a bay color, black mane and tail, his mane tolerably heavy, & near the head inclined to lie on the wrong side ; tail long and slim; a white spot on his forehead ; I am not certain, but think, that one or both of his hind feet white; his rump droops a little, and he is about 5 years old—paces and trots very fast; his neck is long & slim—no brands.

I will pay the above reward and all reasonable charges for the horse delivered here, or five dollars for information so that I can get him. It is supposed he has gone to some point on the Missouri river.

$100 REWARD:

RAN AWAY from the subscriber, living in Boone county, Mo. on Friday the 13th June,

THREE NEGROES,

VIZ DAVE, and JUDY his wife; and JOHN, their son. Dave is about 32 years of age, light color for a full blooded negro—is a good boot and shoe maker by trade : is also a good farm hand. He is about 5 feet 10 or 11 inches high, stout made, and quite an artful, sensible fellow. Had on when he went away, coat and pantaloons of brown woollen jeans, shirt of home made flax linen, and a pair of welted shoes. Judy is rather slender made, about 28 years old, has a very light complexion for a negro ; had on a dress made of flax linen, striped with copperas and blue ; is a first rate house servant and seamstress, and a good spinner, and is very full of affectation when spoken to. John is 9 years old, very likely and well grown ; is remarkably light colored for a negro, and is cross-eyed. Had on a pair of brown jeans pantaloons, bleached flax linen shirt, and red flannel one under it, and a new straw hat.

I will give the above reward and all reasonable expenses, if secured any where out of the State, so that I can get them again, or $50 if taken within the State—$30 for Dave alone, and $20 for Judy and John, and the same in proportion out of the state. The above mentioned clothing was all they took with them from home, but it is supposed he had $30 or $40 in cash with him, so that he may buy and exchange their clothing.

WILLIAM LIENTZ.

Boone county, Mo. June 17, 1834:   52-2

VALUABLE PROPERTY
IN FAYETTE,
For Sale.

THE subscriber, finding it inconvenient to pay that personal attention to his property in the Town of Fayette, which it requires, offers the same for sale, on reasonable terms, for Cash, or on a credit of one and two years. It consists of a Handsome and Convenient Dwelling H

Runaway slave advertisement. *(State Historical Society of Missouri)*

times they were ordered to live together by the master. As far as whites were concerned, the sale of one or the other of the marriage partners ended the relationship. The law never recognized slave marriages. It considered them merely moral agreements with no legal force. After the Civil War, Missouri required all ex-slaves in the state who were living together as man and wife to be remarried "legally."

Restraints on Slaves

Punishments and Restrictions. Slaves were further degraded by laws that divided them from the rest of society. Punishments were barbarous. The general crudeness of frontier justice was made even worse by the slavemaster's fear of rebellious or disobedient slaves. Missouri slaves were not generally treated as inhumanely as were the slaves who lived in the deep South. Still, a slaveowner who was surrounded by free territory on three sides (Illinois, Iowa, and Kansas) was prompted to take strict precautions to keep his bondsmen secure.

Missouri's statutes contained numerous restrictions directed against blacks. They prohibited slaves from carrying arms without a license from the justice of the peace. If a gun was found on a slave, it would be taken away and he would be given thirty-nine lashes on his bare back. This was part of an attempt to protect the master and community against slave uprisings. Slaves found guilty of crimes such as conspiracy, rebellion, or murder were to be put to death.

The owner had a great deal of discretion in the punishment of his slaves. Often a slave was punished in the presence of other slaves so that the master could provide a dramatic lesson of what happened to disobedient slaves. The most frequent punishment consisted of a whipping. The usual instrument was a wooden handle attached to a flat piece of leather belting about a foot and a half long, an inch and a half wide and about a quarter of an inch thick. The number of lashes varied from ten to one hundred. Such a whip could cause blisters, frequently drawing blood, and sometimes leaving permanent scars. Occasionally slaves were beaten with sticks or anything else that might come to the master's hand. Usually, however, the master tried to avoid permanently marking a slave. His reason for this was not so much the result of humaneness as it was a desire to protect his economic investment. A scarred slave would be regarded by a prospective buyer as mean, vicious, or having made attempts to escape. His potential value would be lessened accordingly.

Slaves were forbidden to have sexual relations with white women. Blacks or mulattoes who assaulted or attempted to assault a white woman would be killed or mutilated, often by castration. Rape of a black woman by a white man was less serious in the eyes of the law, however. Sexual assault of a slave woman by a white man was not considered an offense against the woman: it was only a case of trespassing on the master's "property"! Slaves who offered resistance to their owners and overseers could receive thirty-nine stripes. Bondsmen guilty of striking a white person, except in self-defense, were to be punished at the discretion of the justice of the peace. The punishment was not to exceed thirty-nine lashes. Thirty-nine lashes was also the penalty to be suffered by slaves for disturbing church service by "noise, riotous or disorderly conduct. . . ." Any person providing liquor to a slave was to suffer twenty-five lashes on his bare back and be committed to jail. Blacks were even declared to be incompetent as witnesses in legal cases involving whites. They could, however, witness against each other.

By 1847, Missouri slaveowners were extremely fearful of slave insurrections. Convinced that slaves rebelled because they were reading abolitionist literature, they sought to stop rebellions by making it impossible for blacks to learn to read. They sponsored an ordinance specifically prohibiting the education of blacks. Anyone operating a school for Negroes or mulattoes or teaching reading or writing to any Negro or mulatto in Missouri could be punished by a fine of not less than five hundred dollars and sentenced up to six months in jail. This was clearly a law to protect the master and the community against possible slave uprisings such as those led by Denmark Vesey, Nat Turner, and slaves in the southern states.

The Slave Patrols. One of the most important institutions established to ensure the safety of the slaveowners and the community was the system of the slave patrols. Missouri authorized each county to set up its own patrols in 1823. This legislation was designed to ensure against slave plots and insurrection by making sure that the slaves were not traveling abroad at night without their master's consent. Patrols also visited the slave quarters to guarantee that there were no unlawful assemblies of slaves. Thirty-nine lashes was the punishment for such illegal meetings if the patrol took the slave before the justice of the peace; but without the master's permission, punishment by the "patterollers," as the slaves called them, was limited to ten.

As the intensity of the antislavery struggle increased in the years immediately preceding the Civil War, strenuous local laws were passed to control the slaves. In most Missouri cities all blacks without a pass had to be off the street at nine o'clock at night unless on business for their master. Special permission had to be secured from the master for all special meetings, and all such persons had to be home by ten o'clock. Passes were good for twenty-four hours only, and the city constable had to see that meetings were orderly.

Compensation of patrol members varied. Sometimes they received no pay, other than the satisfaction of keeping blacks "in their place." Occasionally slaveowners served as patrollers. Often, however, patrols were made up of the riffraff of the white community, young men who excelled in the sport of having fun with the "niggers." In Cole County, patrolmen were paid eight cents an hour in 1851 and twenty-five cents an hour in 1852. Pay for patrolmen apparently increased as fear engendered by the antislavery movement intensified. Still, five members of the Jefferson City patrol served for the paltry sum of $28.50 for a year's work. Patrol members and the slaves regarded each other from different points of view. The slaves feared the patrol, which was frequently made up of lower-class whites who often took undue advantage of blacks, especially of the women and girls. To many patrolmen, their duties were a form of amusement.

The Slave Trade

Selling Slaves Down South. The "intractable" slave always had one major fear that haunted him continuously: the prospect of being sold away from his family, especially "down South." This was the ultimate legal form of social control open to the slavemaster. It was also the most brutal.

Slave marriages meant little, at least to whites. Husbands were separated from wives, mothers and fathers from children, and even children were sold apart, never to see one another again. Slavemasters rarely allowed compassion and sentiment to interfere with their opportunity to turn a profit. That, after all, was what slavery was all about: making a profit, and keeping blacks in a state of total submission, insofar as that was possible.

The almost insatiable demand for black slaves in the South meant that there was always a buyer from that region ready to purchase a Missouri slave. Several slave dealers carried on the trade in Missouri, buying and selling blacks for the cotton, rice, sugar, and indigo fields of the South. St. Louis was the largest slave mart in the state. Slave dealers there advertised in various counties for salable slaves. In 1845, W. Edgerton, a St. Louis dealer, advertised as follows in the *Jefferson Inquirer:*

> The undersigned proposes remaining a few weeks in this city for the purpose of purchasing a few Negro slaves. Persons having young slaves for sale will find this a favorable opportunity to sell. His rooms are in the national hotel.

St. Louis companies such as Blakey and McAfee kept an agent in the state capital in the early 1850s, offering "highest prices for Negroes of every description." They boasted of their facilities as being "well suited for the boarding and safe keeping of Negroes sent to this market for sale." Competing with them was yet another St. Louis company, Bolton, Dickens and Company. In 1853 the latter firm advertised in the *Jefferson Examiner* for one thousand slaves.

Slavebreeding. Did slaveholders responding to such advertisements follow the lead of their Virginia, Kentucky, Maryland, and other slaveholding brethren in breeding slaves for the market? According to one authority on black slavery, Professor U. B. Phillips, the South shunned this practice. However, Frederick Bancroft, after more than thirty years of research, argued against the Phillips thesis in his *Slave Trading in the Old South.* He found that between 1830 and 1860, Virginia alone exported nearly 300,000 slaves to the New South, a very profitable business indeed. Black men were further dehumanized by being turned into studs to breed offspring for the cotton fields.

None of the slave states admitted the breeding of slaves, and the question of Missouri's involvement in that practice remains debatable. Still, William Wells Brown, an escaped slave who became an anti-slavery speaker and novelist, argued that slavebreeding took place in Missouri, and that the children born of such unions were sold down South. And a former slave claimed that his master "used to have me come over and father children; you know, I was big and strong and made big strong slaves." Frequent advertisements of slaves for sale lend strength to the belief in the rise of Missouri as a slavebreeding state for the lower South.

Although the body of the slave could be severely restrained, battered, used, and abused, his spirit often remained free, however. Slaves responded to the inhumanity of their captivity in a variety of ways, often quite creatively, as we shall see in the next chapter.

SUGGESTED READINGS

Two of the best works on slavery done recently in Missouri remain in the form of dissertations written by university students for doctoral degrees. These dissertations can be ordered directly from University Microfilms International, 300 N. Zeeb Road, Ann Arbor, Michigan 48106: Donnie D. Bellamy, "Slavery, Emancipation, and Racism in Missouri, 1850-1865" (University of Missouri—Columbia, 1970);

Robert William Duffner, "Slavery in Missouri River Counties, 1820-1865" (University of Missouri—Columbia, 1974).

One of the most promising recent trends in the study of slavery has been the interest shown in localized studies. The following articles are good examples: Lyle W. Dorsett, "Slaveholding in Jackson County, Missouri," *Bulletin* [Missouri Historical Society], XX (October 1963), pages 33-34; George R. Lee, "Slavery and Emancipation in Lewis County, Missouri," *Missouri Historical Review*, LXV (April 1971), pages 294-317; James William McGettigan, Jr., "Boone County Slaves: Sales, Estate Divisions and Families, 1820-1865," Parts I and II, *Missouri Historical Review*, LXXII (January and April 1978), pages 176-197 and 271-295; Philip V. Scarpino, "Slavery in Callaway County, Missouri: 1845-1855," Parts I and II, *Missouri Historical Review*, LXXI (October and April 1976-77), pages 22-43 and 266-283; and W. Sherman Savage, "Contest Over Slavery Between Illinois and Missouri," *Journal of Negro History*, XXVIII (July 1943), pages 311-345.

3

The Slave Strikes Back:
The Reaction to Bondage

The Missouri slave was not the docile, contented, willing, happy "Sambo" that many masters and historians claimed he was. All of the available evidence suggests that black slaves hated their servile role in the white man's world and that they were quite creative in their protests against the way of life imposed upon them. Their ways of protest were many, both nonviolent and violent.

Slave Revolts

The Danger and Difficulty of Revolt. The protest that whites feared the most was slave rebellion. The strength of numbers meant that at least temporarily the rebelling slaves were unstoppable, able to slay and overcome the unorganized resistance of an individual master or even a small white community. Black rebellion began with the Africans captured by white slavers and shipped to the new world. It was not uncommon for the Africans to rise in mutiny against the shipmaster while on the ocean voyage and to attempt to kill the entire crew, in their effort to return home to Africa. Those who survived the ocean voyage continued to struggle.

Once the slave was sold in America and settled with his or her master, the chances of joint rebellion were lessened, but still real. Many slaveowners did not treat their slaves so brutally as to inspire rebellion or other retaliation, but even the kindliest slaveowner feared that his slaves might someday rebel. This fear was heightened by the knowledge of rebellion elsewhere in the United States. In 1831, Nat Turner and sixty to seventy other slaves rebelled in Virginia, killing Turner's owner and nearly sixty other whites.

But slave rebellions were doomed to failure because the whites had superior forces: the Virginia militia captured and killed twenty of the rebels, including Turner, and whites in the area reacted by killing another hundred innocent slaves. Individual slaveowners, including those in Missouri, feared that they, like Turner's owner, would be slaughtered before white forces could be gathered. As we have seen, the restrictive and harsh Black Codes were aimed at repression, as was the denial of education—Turner had been an educated preacher, who believed God had given him a mission to free the slaves.

Slave Revolts in Missouri. There is no evidence that an armed revolt of slaves ever occurred in Missouri—indeed, from our vantage point today we can see that the chances of success were less in Missouri where blacks were a much smaller percentage of the population than in the deep South. There was, however, at least one narrow miss in the state.

In November 1849, the McCutchen farm in Lewis County was the scene of a potential insurrection that was barely nipped in time. McCutchen was awakened one night by voices coming from a kitchen that was separated from his house by a passageway. Soon a slave from the adjoining farm owned by John Miller approached McCutchen, asking for guns. The black man moved toward the gun rack, at which point McCutchen called to his slaves for help. The slaves failed to respond and McCutchen took his family, fleeing into the night. He went to the Miller farm where the two slaveowners decided to send out a general alert.

By morning thirty armed whites were approaching the McCutchen farm. They found that slaves from four families had barricaded themselves in the house. The slaves were armed with three guns, butcher knives, and clubs. The slaveowners ordered the blacks to surrender. One of the slaves, John, apparently the leader, came out. Instead of surrendering, however, he made at Captain Blair with his corn knife. Someone in the crowd shot the slave on John Miller's order, but the slave kept coming at Blair. A second shot killed him.

Having seen their leader killed, the other slaves surrendered. Ultimately, all of them were sold South; neither Miller nor McCutchen wanted to give these slaves another chance to carry out a successful revolt. For months after the aborted rebellion, controversy raged in Lewis County about what had gotten into the Miller and McCutchen slaves. Some argued that the slave woman Lin was behind the whole thing. She was alleged to have concocted a potion of coffee and tea that she gave to the slaves to make them powerful. Others blamed Henry, Lin's ten-year-old grandson, who had visions of all whites being dead. Still others blamed United States Senator Thomas Hart Benton who had been making antislavery speeches in the state the previous spring. Many believed that whites from a place called Gregory's Landing were also involved. Supposedly, they were going to help the rebellious slaves escape, although some argued the whites' real goal was to get the slaves on board a boat and sell them down South.

Individual Protest: Crime Against Whites

Destroying the Master's Property. Although Missouri slaves rarely united to rebel violently against their masters, many did strike out in other ways at the institution of slavery and the whites who enforced it. Because slavery was basically a profit-motivated economic system, slaves sometimes sought to make slavery as unprofitable as possible by breaking the master's tools, crippling or killing his livestock, and by personally slowing down the pace of their work. Others feigned illness or ignorance of how to do a particular job, allowed the animals to stray, or pulled up plants instead of weeds.

Tony, a Boone County slave, took out his frustrations on his master's livestock. He had been accused of stealing a hog. He worked at a university laboratory as a janitor, so in anger he stole a bottle of acid and poured it on his master's mules. Following his arrest, he confessed to the deed. The court convicted Tony and sentenced him to thirty-nine lashes on his bare back. He was taken before a meat market, where observers could readily watch, and then strung up and whipped. Every blow, it is said, drew blood or raised a blister. Later he was freed by his master and went to Iowa.

In 1857, another slave named Gilbert allegedly cut the throat of a mare belonging to Charles Crane. Gilbert was brought to trial and convicted. Fortunately for Gilbert, the Missouri Supreme Court later voided his conviction on a legal technicality.

Stealing or "Taking." Stealing by slaves was also common practice. To the slave, "taking" from his master or any whites was regarded as a form of compensation for his unpaid labor. A Missouri slave named Joe was arrested for stealing a fiddle valued at one dollar and other goods having a total value of two dollars. He was tried before a justice of the peace, convicted, and whipped. Another such crime occurred in Callaway County in 1841. A slave named Carter broke into a store at night and took about sixteen dollars. He was brought to trial in that county and found guilty. His punishment was not mentioned, but his master was obliged to pay all costs.

Arson. Arson was a popular form of slave protest. Arsonists could start fires in buildings belonging to whites who had inspired their wrath, and the whites would have a difficult time fixing the blame on a particular individual. In Howard County in 1847, a slave owned by Mr. Reed was arrested for burning his master's property. He was convicted and sentenced to be sent out of the state for twenty years.

Nine years later, a female slave belonging to Mr. Towler in the same county was accused of burning a stable belonging to a Mr. Phillips. The latter brought suit against Towler for damages. During the trial the slave had been allowed to testify, although Towler's counsel had objected to the use of her testimony. Towler meanwhile died, and the suit was continued against the administrator of his estate.

In 1844, a slave named Sam was said to have entered the house of John G. Koenig of Jefferson County, struck him with a club, robbed him, and set fire to the house. This case was unusual because although Sam was a black slave and the crime was a shocking one, he was acquitted for lack of evidence. That judgment was made even though Sam had in his possession some of Koenig's belongings.

Rape. Other slaves struck out at their masters by daring to engage in what whites considered to be one of the most heinous of crimes: sexual relations with white women. Elaborate legal codes had been devised to protect white womanhood from the slaves. A slave found guilty of raping a white female could expect to be castrated or even killed. But the slave who commonly saw his women violated by the master or other whites, often, despite the risk, attempted to rape a white female. In some instances, white women offered their bodies to slaves, feeling secure in the knowledge that if they were caught, they could always claim that the slave was the aggressor and that his testimony to the contrary would never be accepted by a court of law. One should recall that the rape of a slave woman, by contrast, was seen only as a trespass upon the master's property. Indeed, even the rape of a white woman by a white man was less serious, resulting, in most cases, in a five- to ten-year prison sentence.

Individual Protest: Murder

The most extreme form of protest against enslavement was murder. On occasion, a Missouri slave sought to break the shackles of bondage by killing his or her master. In 1848, Patsy, a Boone County slave, was convicted of attempting to poison her mistress by putting arsenic in her milk. She was sentenced to receive thirty-nine lashes on her bare back "well laid on" and to be jailed for sixty days. Seven years later another slave tried to poison her master's child; she too was sentenced to thirty-nine lashes "well laid on."

In 1838 a slave woman, Fannie, allegedly murdered two boys belonging to William Prewitt of Lincoln County. The boys had received permission to pick some peaches in an orchard owned by Fannie's master. That was the last time the boys were seen alive. Four days later the sheriff arrested Fannie, her husband, and their young son. The officer subsequently resorted to threats of dire punishment to force Elick, Fannie's son, to incriminate his mother as the murderer. According to Elick, the sheriff and another man threatened to hang him unless he turned informer. Strung up, with a rope around his neck, the terrified youth accused his mother of killing the boys when they came for peaches. Elick made that statement, however, only after the sheriff had assured him that the remainder of the family had already been hanged. Although Fannie was convicted and sentenced to be hanged, no concrete incriminatory evidence was found against her. A stick with what was supposed to be blood and the two naked bodies of the victims were all the evidence against Fannie. However, the brutal manner in which a child was forced to condemn his mother was too much for the Supreme Court of Missouri to accept. The court reversed the decision.

Sometimes a slave was driven by fear of punishment to commit murder. An example of this spontaneous reaction to the threat of a whipping occurred in Boone County in 1837. James T. Paints had hired William Robinson's slave, Joe, for the purpose of splitting rails. Paints sent Joe to the woods alone. Upon his return, Paints asked him how many rails he had split. Paints later inspected Joe's work and discovered the slave had lied concerning the number of rails split. The following day Paints accompanied Joe to the woods where the two began splitting rails. When they sat down to rest, Paints began telling the slave how severe the punishment was for lying, implying that Joe was going to be whipped. Joe seized an ax and struck Paints upon the head, killing him instantly. He then hid the body and fled. He was later arrested, confessed to the crime, and was lodged in the county jail to await trial. The verdict was guilty and the slave was sentenced to death by hanging. The sentence was carried out on November 13, 1837.

In 1860, Miss Susan Jemima Barnes had remained at home while the rest of her family went for a visit. Upon returning they found her dead upon the floor. Practically all of her facial and cranial bones had been crushed. An examination revealed that she probably had been stabbed a number of times as well. After the coroner's inquest had been held, suspicion was thrown upon Teney, a female slave, who it was charged, was usually impudent and insolent unless a white man was around. Teney denied the accusation at first but later confessed when one of her bloodstained dresses was found hidden in a cornfield. The county constable had started to Fulton with Teney in custody when he was overtaken by an outraged mob. The mob threatened the constable and forced him to turn Teney over to them. They immediately hanged her from a nearby tree.

In the case of the *State* v. *Celia, a Slave,* it was found that Celia, a Negro slave girl of fourteen, was purchased by an elderly farmer of Callaway County. The farmer was some seventy years of age and a grandfather in 1850. There was some feeling that the wealthy farmer, a large landowner, and an active churchman, may have forced himself upon the girl sexually as he took her home following the purchase in Audrain County. At any rate, it is known that he visited her cabin fairly regularly for the purpose of satisfying his sexual desires, and that Celia did not view these visits favorably. Celia lived with her children in a cabin very close to her master's house. On the night of June 23, 1855, the farmer again visited the cabin of Celia, despite her repeated warnings to stay away. Celia had earlier told her master that she "would hurt him if he did not quit forcing her while she was sick." Celia had been pregnant for some months. This time when the master advanced toward her, she struck him on the head with a stick, killing him. She then burned his body in the fireplace of her cabin, carrying out the ashes the next morning.

A search of the ashes by local officials revealed buttons and bits of bone. An inquest was held and Celia was jailed until her trial in October. Celia was found guilty and sentenced to be hanged on November 16, 1855. Her counsel requested a new trial but was denied. In the meantime, Celia escaped from the Fulton jail but was recaptured. Her execution was delayed until the birth of her stillborn child. Rumor had it that the child had been fathered by the farmer whom she had murdered. On December 13, 1855, she was taken to the gallows and there hanged at the young age of nineteen.

Crimes Against Other Slaves

Frustration and Violence. Slaves also committed crimes against each other. In some instances, slaves who felt powerless to rebel against the oppressive life imposed upon them by a racist society vented their frustrations by inflicting violence on other slaves. Violence committed against another slave was seen more as a crime against the master's property than against the victim. When a slave killed another slave or a free Negro, punishment was usually by whipping or else the owners themselves settled the matter out of court. For example, Lorine, a slave woman who possessed an ugly temper, fought with, and threw Marianne, another slave, into a hole she had chopped in the ice for fishing. Another slave saved Marianne from drowning, but the furious Lorine grabbed and threw her into a fire, burning her severely. Lorine's punishment was one hundred lashes to be administered on two separate days. Later, a Clay County slave who murdered another slave and was convicted was given thirty lashes and sold out of the state.

Self-mutilation and Suicide. Slaves sometimes turned violent hands upon themselves to cripple the system further. The purpose was to depreciate their value, make slave-keeping more unprofitable and avoid being sold down South. Women might even kill their offspring. A case in point was Margaret of Cole County. Her master found her one morning in 1848 foaming at the mouth. Upon talking with her, the master believed that the slave had miscarried. However, a search revealed part of the baby's body had been eaten by hogs. A blood-stained knife was found nearby. Margaret was arrested and indicted for murder. A doctor testified the knife had been used to sever the umbilical cord; the court found Margaret guilty, although no mention was made of her punishment.

Other slave mothers reacted violently when their children were sold away. One instance occurred in 1834, in Marion County, Missouri. A slave trader bought three small children from a planter. The mother became so violent that she had to be tied up. During the night she broke her bonds and killed her sons with an ax, chopping off their heads. She then turned the same instrument on herself, ending her own life. Reportedly, the slave trader's only comments reflected his sorrow at having lost a financial investment. Another Boone County slave tried to thwart his master's selling him South by cutting the fingers off his left hand.

The prospect of husband and wife being separated induced a suicide on at least one occasion. In April 1835, a slave was informed that he had been sold South without his wife. He responded by hanging himself, apparently preferring death to separation from his spouse.

Runaways

Escape. Hundreds of other slaves, simply by running away, at a single

Runaway slave crossing river on horseback. *(State Historical Society of Missouri)*

stroke deprived their master of his investment in his human property, as well as the economic gain expected from it. To add insult to injury, the absconding slave frequently carried away some of his master's property. Masters often placed advertisements in newspapers for runaway slaves, to alert other whites to assist in recapturing their escaped slaves. These advertisements generally carried a description of the runaway, including name, age, occupation, clothing, and any identifying scars or physical characteristics.

This was the case of a Boone County slave, Betsy. The advertisement of July 7, 1832 read, "$100 reward. Lost on night of 6 and 7 of April last. . .A Negro woman and her four children. Her name is Betsy. Complexion is yellow, with a good supply of clothing for a servant. Her bedding, box, cooking utensils, etc. The children range from 9 months to 6 years of age." The master feared that the same people who had carried off her husband Tom had taken away Betsy.

A runaway in 1840 who lived twenty miles from Jefferson City had the good sense to put as much distance between himself and his owner as possible. He "rode away on [his master's] sorrel horse with two white hind feet, 15 hands high and somewhat white in the forehead." The slave was identified as being "23 years old, slender, yellow, having broad teeth set far apart, scar on one cheek and the ball of one eye yellow." From the description of the horse, the owner seemed to be as interested in the loss of the animal as in the loss of the slave.

One black Missouri runaway who later became famous was William Wells Brown. Brown, who had worked on the Mississippi River boats, ran away, became an ardent abolitionist, received a college education, and lectured extensively abroad. He wrote a letter on November 23, 1849, from London to his former master, Captain Enoch Price of St. Louis, challenging the law that had made him Price's slave. The letter, published in the *Libertarian* on September 14, 1849, declared that

> The United States had disfranchised me and declared that I am not a citizen, but a chattel: her Constitution dooms me to be your slave. But while I feel grieved that I am maligned and driven from my own country, I rejoice that in this land I am regarded as a man.

The Underground Railroad. Many slavemasters felt that slave escapes were being facilitated by the Underground Railroad, a system which saw sympathetic whites provide way stations for runaways who were fleeing North. Allegedly, St. Louis was a central depot for the Underground Railroad, with a home on Spoede Road and the Helfenstein plantation in Webster Groves serving as important stopping places. Although it seems likely that the Underground Railroad did help some Missouri slaves to escape, it is unlikely that it had the effect on Missouri slavery that contemporary masters believed.

Religion. Many slaveowners did not treat their slaves brutally, but even when the slave was not abused, he was still a captive, held against his will. While he might not turn to violence, there were still other forms of protest available to him. Often slaves turned to religion and found relief believing in a God who would reward their patient suffering in an afterlife. Nowhere was this sentiment better expressed than in the spiritual which spoke of heaven as the slave's real home:

> This world is not my home.
> This world is not my home.
> This world's a howling wilderness,
> This world is not my home.[1]

In most instances, slaves were forced to worship with their masters so they could be watched. Often back in the slave quarters, however, they had their own religious service which might include the ridiculing of their masters. Sometimes they expressed the hope that a just God would "take care of" the whites who abused them, as was the case in this song:

> My ole mistress promised me
> Before she died she would set me free. . . .
> Now she's dead and gone to hell,
> I hope the devil will burn her well.[2]

Songs, Stories, and the Community. Indeed, songs and stories were two important ways in which black slaves could try to insulate themselves from the harshest realities of slave life. They could recount to each other the unlimited exploits of Brer Rabbit, who, though smaller and weaker than most other animals, always managed to defeat his "masters" by cunning and trickery. Such exploits were also celebrated in songs sung out of the master's hearing:

> I fooled Old Master seven years,
> Fooled the overseer three.
> Hand me down my banjo,
> And I'll tickle your bel-lee.[3]

Slaves might even indulge in criticism of one of their own who had been assigned the responsibility of supervising them:

> O, de ole nigger-driver!
>   O, gwine away!
> Fust ting my mammay tell me,
>   O, gwine away!
>
> Tell me 'bout de nigger-driver,
>   O, gwine away!
> Nigger-driver second devil,
>   O, gwine away![4]

The Slave Community. Many slaves realized that their survival demanded a togetherness, a sense of community, that would allow them to draw upon each other's emotional and psychological strength. Contrary to what historians once supposed, for example, the black family was strong during slave times. It was an island of familiarity and love in a sea of hostility and hate.

Thus blacks responded to slavery in a variety of ways: sometimes they protested vigorously against it, either violently or nonviolently, and at other times they simply turned inward and tried to make the best of a bad situation. Whatever the case, virtually all of them yearned to be free, a status which, as we shall see in the next chapter, could be attained by only a fortunate few.

NOTES

1. William E. Barton, *Old Plantation Hymns* (Boston, 1899), page 9.

2. Thomas W. Talley, *Negro Folk Rhymes* (New York, 1922), page 25.

3. Norman R. Yetman, ed., *Voices from Slavery* (New York, 1970), page 253.

4. Quoted in Thomas Wentworth Higginson, *Army Life in a Black Regiment* (Michigan, 1960), page 171.

SUGGESTED READINGS

Most of the studies on slavery have to be read with care because of the tendency to view the institution from the perspective of the master rather than the slave. Until recently the reaction of the slave to his bondage has been largely ignored by scholars.

The most extensive treatment of violent resistance to slavery is Herbert Aptheker, *American Negro Slave Revolts* (New York, 1943). Two recent studies that devote much attention to the slave's nonviolent protest against slavery are Eugene D. Genovese, *Roll, Jordan, Roll: The World the Slave Made* (New York, 1974) and Lawrence W. Levine, *Black Culture and Black Consciousness* (New York, 1977).

Other recent successful efforts to tell more of the slave's side of the story include Stanley Feldstein, *Once a Slave: The Slave's View of Slavery* (New York, 1971) and John Blassingame, *The Slave Community* (New York, 1972). George P. Rawick, *The American Slave: A Composite Autobiography* (Westport, Connecticut, 1971), is a multivolume reprinting of the interviews with ex-slaves, conducted in the 1930s by the Works Progress Administration. It includes many Missouri interviews.

William Wells Brown was a runaway Missouri slave whose experiences are retold in his *Narrative of William Wells Brown, a Fugitive Slave* (1848), reprinted with an introduction by Larry Gara (Reading, Massachusetts, 1969). The sad case of the slave Celia is detailed in Hugh P. Williamson, "The State Against Celia, a Slave," *Midwest Journal*, VIII (Spring-Fall 1956), pages 408-420.

4

Slaves Without Masters:
Free Blacks Before the Civil War

The black men and women who finally gained their freedom at the end of the Civil War in Missouri were not the first black freedmen of the state. A free Negro class, distinct and separate from either whites or slaves, existed throughout the period of slavery in Missouri, although the distinction between free blacks and slaves was often vague.

There were approximately 488,000 free blacks and 4,000,000 slaves in the United States in 1860 on the eve of the Civil War. Free blacks caused concern in all slave states, and reactions to the problem revealed a uniform response. This was as true for Missouri, with slightly more than 100,000 slaves, as for South Carolina and Virginia, both with more than 400,000 slaves. But Missouri's free black population, like its slave population, remained smaller than either South Carolina's or Virginia's. In 1860, Missouri had 3,572 free blacks, compared to nearly 10,000 in South Carolina, 58,000 in Virginia, and 83,900 in Maryland. The larger the slave population, the harsher the treatment of the free blacks.

Free Blacks in a Slave Society

The Threat to Slavery. The presence of free blacks in a slave society threatened to undermine the very foundation upon which slavery was built. The continuation of the slave system was based upon the assumption that whites would exercise indisputable control over blacks. Freedmen, regardless of the theoretical rights and equalities which freedom implied, could not be allowed to subvert that system by acting as if they were as good as whites!

It was necessary, therefore, for Missouri and other slave states to conduct a campaign of suppression against free blacks in order to "keep them in their place." That place was a position inferior to the position of white men. Free blacks had to be maintained as a separate and distinct class so that, among other things, they could be more easily observed. Whites were convinced that free blacks instigated many of the attempts made by southern slaves to break the bonds of servitude. Consequently, the more expressive freedmen were, the more fearful whites became of their holding "tumultous and unlawful meetings" out of which would come secret plots and conspiracies that would lead to slave insurrections.

This widespread fear of the free black class as a potential threat to slavery manifested itself in laws and social customs designed to institutionalize black, rather than merely slave, inferiority and subjugation. South Carolina, for example, made very little legal distinction between slaves and free blacks. Any free black caught trespassing would be adjudged guilty of a misdemeanor. He could be punished at the discretion of the court, so long as the court did not kill or maim him. Additional laws enacted to control free blacks in South Carolina included laws against employing them as clerks or salesmen and even a law forbidding whites to gamble with free Negroes. Likewise, in Virginia, legislators made it clear that free blacks would have few privileges forbidden to slaves. Blacks were prohibited from testifying against whites, being taught to read and write, or carrying firearms.

Restrictions on Missouri's Free Blacks. Free blacks in Missouri faced equally stringent legislation. First of all, the state tried to make it difficult for blacks to gain their freedom. A black person was not considered legally free without a deed of manumission, written and certified by the state or county authorities. Such legal red tape hindered the ability of a slave to gain his or her freedom. Children fathered by a free man, black or white, remained slaves unless their mother was also free; children always followed the status of the mother. In this manner, additions were made to the slaveowner's property.

As early as 1817, the territorial government of Missouri passed an act which curtailed the ability of free blacks to travel and gather in meetings, and thus hoped to curtail slave insurrections. As a result of this law, it became illegal for freedmen to assemble even for purposes of education, although, for the moment, there was no decree against the education of blacks. In 1847, however, the Missouri General Assembly passed a law forbidding blacks to be taught even the rudiments of reading and writing. This act, too, was a reflection of a slaveholder's fear that literacy might lead to rebellion. Nat Turner, it was argued, would never have led a slave rebellion in Virginia had his mind not been opened to the world of freedom by the materials he read.

Other statutory attempts in Missouri to subjugate freedmen included a law of 1825 which declared blacks to be incompetent as witnesses in legal cases involving whites. That law indicates the low esteem in which free blacks were held: it permitted slaves, who were considered totally irresponsible before the law, to testify against them. In 1835 it was declared illegal for a free black or mulatto to possess a firearm "or weapon of any kind," without first having acquired a license from a justice of the peace in the county where he resided. The license, of course, could be granted and revoked at the discretion of the justice.

Another Type of Slavery

Binding Out. One of the most restrictive laws enacted against free blacks in Missouri was passed in 1835. It required county courts to bring before their benches all free Negroes and mulattoes between the ages of seven and twenty-one years and bind them out to be apprentices or servants—in short, to enslave them by another name. It was further legislated that no colored apprentice should be placed in the company of a free white worker, except by the consent of the parent or guardian of the said white apprentice. To place a black man alongside a white man in the learning of the same trade was considered a dangerous first step toward the emancipation of the slave.

The Free License. Fear of free blacks manifested itself in another way in 1835. In that year, the Missouri legislature tried to restrict the movement of free blacks into and within the state. The legislature declared that in order to reside in a Missouri county a free Negro had to obtain a license from the county court. The license was, in effect, a permit to remain in the county so long as one behaved. To get the permit, the black applicant had either to post a bond ranging from one hundred to one thousand dollars or get some white person to act as security for him. The license granted to Celia James in 1847 was typical. The Cole County court ordered that "Celia James be and she is hereby licensed to remain in the State of Missouri during good behavior, and there-

Dred Scott. *(Missouri Historical Society, St. Louis)*

upon she enters into bond in the sum of three hundred dollars with John D. Curry as Security which is approved and ordered to be filed."

The whole question of free licenses keenly reflects the attitude of policymakers toward blacks in general and free blacks in particular. The burden of proof always rested upon the black person, for, as one historian has written, "color raised the presumption of slavery." It was assumed that all blacks were slaves until they could offer proof to the contrary. A freedman brought before a justice of the peace, who was unable to persuade the court that he was free, could be jailed as a common runaway or sold back into slavery.

In 1846 the constitutionality of this pernicious free license law was sustained by Judge John M. Krum of the St. Louis Circuit Court. Krum denied the claim that blacks were citizens of the United States "in the meaning of the word as expressed in the constitution." His decision offered a portent of things to come. His argument followed the same line of reasoning used in 1857 by the United States Supreme Court in rejecting Dred Scott's attempt to insist upon equal protection of the laws of the United States. It meant, in effect, that free blacks had no rights that whites were obligated to respect.

How Slaves Obtained Their Freedom

Escape and Purchase. Despite these legal restrictions and other obstacles, the free black class increased in a number of ways. One way was escape, a method of gaining one's freedom dealt with in the previous chapter. Generally, however, a slave gained his freedom only after the master agreed. According to Harrison Trexler, an authority on slavery in Missouri, there were, generally speaking, two motives that entered into the act of liberating a slave: financial consideration and sentiment.

Most frequently, slaves purchased their freedom. This meant that the cash payment they offered the master had to be worth more than he would receive from their continued servitude. The cost of freedom depended upon several variables, among them sex, age, health, skills possessed by the slave, and the availability of a ready market for slaves. The price of freedom varied. Occasionally, it was as low as two hundred dollars, as it was when Jonathan Ramsey manumitted his slave girl Chaney in 1839. Mr. Ramsey, however, indicated that the money was not his only motive and that he was also prompted by "benevolence and humanity."

Often, however, the purchase price ran high. In 1857, for example, forty-year-old John Lane paid twelve hundred dollars for his freedom. Lane was perhaps the most self-sufficient black man in the capital city and was to remain a prominent figure in black affairs in the state for another thirty years. He was one of the few free blacks who held any property in Cole County during the antebellum period. He became, in the early postwar years, one of the strongest supporters of Lincoln Institute, later to become known as Lincoln University. For many years after the Civil War, he and another black man, Howard Barnes, operated a restaurant and hotel that was one of the most popular dining places in Jefferson City.

Purchasing a Family's Freedom. Occasionally, free blacks who were able to purchase their freedom turned around and purchased the freedom of other members of their family. Violet Ramsey, for example, first purchased her freedom by taking in washing and ironing. She then began to save money for the purchase of her enslaved husband Elijah. Ultimately, both of them pooled their resources and purchased the freedom of their son, Elijah, Jr., or "Cudge."

Other slaves took advantage of the California Gold Rush. A Cole County slave named Joe traveled to California with his master in 1849. While there, he earned enough money to pay his master sixteen hundred dollars for his freedom. He also earned enough (two thousand dollars) to buy the freedom of his wife and children. A St. Louis slave, Jesse Hubbard, accompanied his master to California and returned with fifteen thousand dollars. Subsequently, Hubbard purchased his freedom and bought a farm in St. Louis County.

Free Blacks as Slaveowners. Occasionally Missouri's free blacks would themselves become slaveholders. In some instances, their motives were similar to those of their white counterparts: they wanted the use of slave labor to make money. Often, however, their goal was to allow their slaves an opportunity to earn money for self-purchase. One of the most famous of the antebellum free blacks in the state who engaged in this practice was St. Louisan John Berry Meachum.

Meachum was born a slave in Virginia and worked under a skilled craftsman from whom he learned to do carpentry, cabinet-making, and coopering (barrel-making). He earned enough money to purchase his freedom, married, and when his wife's master moved to St. Louis, he pulled up stakes for Missouri. He found employment in St. Louis and was soon able to purchase his wife and children. Meachum's industriousness allowed him to save enough money so that he could begin a barrel factory, which became a school for freedom. Between 1826 and 1836 he purchased approximately twenty slaves whom he employed in his factory until they had learned a trade and saved enough money to buy their freedom.

E. B. Cordell To Deed of Manumission

Know all men by These presents that I Enos B. Cordell of the State of Missouri County of Cole and in consideration of the sum of One Thousand Dollars, to me in hand paid do emancipate liberate and set free from the bonds of servitude [my] negro woman named Julia Brock and do hereby granting and giving [sic] to the said Julia as far as within me [lies] all the rights and privileges of a free person of color.

In testimony whereof I have hereunto set my hand and seal this Fourth day of February one Thousand eight hundred and fifty-eight.
Filed Feb. 20th, 1858
G. A. Parsons, Clerk

                                        E. B. Cordell   Seal

Document of freedom. *(Lincoln University)*

Know all men by these presents that we Sarah Lane; William Wade; George H. Lane; Deverit J. Lane; Will Lane; Johnell Lane; Lorenzo D. Lane; and Elizabeth J. Lane; all of the County of Cole and State of Missouri, for and in consideration of the sum of twelve hundred dollars to us in hand paid by John a negro Slave, in proportion to our respective shares, the receipt of which is hereby acknowledged, and in further consideration of his the said John's good conduct and fidelity have manumitted—emancipate [sic] and by these presents do manumit emancipate and forever set free the said negro slave John, and release him from the service and claim of ourselves and our heirs, said slave John being about forty years old and of a bright mulato complexion with black hair inclined to be straight and about five feet eight inches in height. In testimony whereof we have hereto [set] our hands and seals this twenty-second day of October A. D. 1856

Witness	her
Alg. Bathe	Sarah X Lane (Seal)
H. L. Bruno for	Mark
D. J. L. & L. D. L.	Wm. Wade (Seal)
R. W. Anderson	George H. Lane (Seal)
W. W. L.	D. Jarret Lane (Seal)
W. Wade	D. L. Lane (Seal)
G. H. L.	Wm. M. Lane (Seal)
Dr. L. L.	his
	John X Lane (Seal)
Filed May 25, 1857	Mark
G. H. Parsons, Clerk	his
By R. W. Anderson, D. C.	Lorenzo D.X. Lane (Seal)
	Mark
	E. J. Lane (Seal)

Document of freedom. *(Lincoln University)*

White Resentment. The fact that a number of free blacks were able to rise above the obstacles placed in their paths by a persistently racist society caused Missourians to continue to hate and fear free blacks right down to the Civil War. The clearest manifestation of this hostility was the continuous effort to colonize freedmen outside of the state or even the nation. The American Colonization Society, established by slaveholders in 1816, founded Liberia to rid the country of free blacks. Ironically, an abolitionist might also be a racist. For instance, many Missouri emancipationists were willing to endorse the abolition of slavery in the state only if the freed blacks were transported out of the country. Emancipationists were particularly eager to send Missouri freedmen to Liberia. Most free blacks claimed America as their home, resisted emigration, and the movement in Missouri, as elsewhere, proved a failure.

The Life of the Free Black

Education. We have already seen John Berry Meachum as an illustration of the success of free blacks—a man whose industriousness and ability enabled him to buy his freedom and become a successful businessman. There were other aspects of this man's career which illustrate another facet of Missouri's black heritage: Meachum was actively involved in education as a means to success. Missouri slaveowners feared that a literate free black class would be rebellious, and this had prompted the enactment in 1847 of legislation to outlaw education for blacks. Meachum was the force behind one of the most creative and effective efforts to get around that law.

In addition to being a businessman, Meachum was also an ordained minister. He was the founder of the First African Baptist Church of St. Louis, located on Third and Almond Streets. In the years before the legislation of 1847, Meachum was in the forefront of efforts to educate blacks, both slave and free. He constantly encouraged those he taught to view education as the key to their success as freedmen. When opposition to the education of blacks surfaced, Meachum went underground. Initially he taught slaves and free blacks to read and write under the guise of conducting a Sunday School. When whites became aware of what he was doing, he switched tactics. He built a steamboat, equipped it with a library, and anchored it in the middle of the Mississippi River, which was subject to federal, not state, law. Each morning he transported students to his school by means of a skiff and, once having gotten them on board, proceeded to teach them reading, writing, and arithmetic, in defiance of state law. Meachum's "floating" school continued until his death in the late 1850s and became famous throughout the nation.

There were other, if somewhat less dramatic, efforts to educate blacks in antebellum Missouri. Timothy Flint, a northern white missionary minister, conducted a school in St. Charles from 1816 to 1826. White college students at Marion College in northeast Missouri taught blacks in the 1830s and a number of schools for blacks run by St. Louis Catholics operated with varying degrees of success throughout the antebellum period.

Other schools operated by free blacks in the state included one run by the Reverend Tom Henderson in Hannibal. Henderson was a Methodist minister. During the Civil War, his school was taken over by another free black, Blanche K. Bruce, who later became the second black person in the history of the country to serve in the United States Senate. Bruce moved to Mississippi after the war and, in 1874, was elected to the Senate. He was the only black to be elected to a full term in the Senate until the arrival of Edward Brooke of Massachusetts in 1966. The only other black man to serve in the Senate during the nineteenth century, Hiram K. Revels, was also associated with antebellum black education in Missouri. Revels opened a school in St. Louis in 1856, enrolling approximately 150 freedmen and slaves at a cost of one dollar per month per pupil. Revels, when elected to the United States Senate in 1870, was chosen to occupy the seat previously held by Jefferson Davis of Mississippi, the former president of the Confederacy.

The Black Church. One of the most important institutions in the Missouri free black community was the church. The church provided freedmen with a source of stability and social strength in an otherwise hostile society. Additionally, the black churches provided one of the few forums where potential black leaders could develop and refine their leadership skills. Unfortunately, the same sentiment which led blacks to establish their own churches caused whites to fear them. Often, therefore, blacks who wished to worship had to do so in white churches, physically separated from the rest of the congregation.

St. Louis, where nearly half of the state's free blacks resided, was the only place in the state where the black church achieved any measure of success. By 1860 there were three Baptist and two Methodist churches in the city. White anxiety about possible slave rebellions led the Missouri General Assembly to pass a law in 1847 that required a county official to attend all religious services conducted by blacks. Just how strictly that law was enforced is not known.

Occupations. How were these free blacks, who were so hated and feared by whites, able to survive in a competitive Missouri economy?

Freedmen's cabin. (*State Historical Society of Missouri*)

Were they social burdens as their white contemporaries charged? Employment was a problem for free blacks. Some stayed with their masters after receiving their freedom and continued as farm workers or common laborers. Skilled freedmen stood a better chance of getting a job, but even they found employment difficult in rural areas.

Quite naturally, then, free blacks in the state tended to migrate to the city, especially St. Louis. In 1860, the Mound City had 1,500 "free men of color" out of a total free black population of 3,572 in the state. These former slaves worked as waggoners, blacksmiths, carpenters, house servants, cooks, waiters, draymen, stone masons, watchmen, carriage drivers, painters, gardeners, hostlers, stable keepers, store owners, chamber maids, wash women, ironers, and seamstresses.

Throughout the state, free blacks demonstrated their ability to fit into a free society, despite the restrictions placed upon them. In the early days of the state many free blacks became trappers, hunters, mountain men, and leaders of wagon trains going west. Jean Baptiste Pointe DeSable, the founder of Chicago, was a mulatto fur trapper who subsequently settled in St. Charles, Missouri. James P. Beckwourth, another black trapper, accompanied General William Henry Ashley's fur expedition in 1823. He spent four decades as a scout, trapper, trader, explorer, and ranger. Among his many accomplishments, he discovered the famous pass over the Sierra Nevada that bears his name.

Another free black Missourian who caught the western expansion fever was George Bush. Bush left Missouri for Oregon and returned several times to lead settlers to that region. He also helped finance white settlers who were migrating there. Bush later moved to what would become the state of Washington and helped establish the United States' claim to that territory. Subsequently, his son was selected to serve as a member of the first legislature in the state of Washington. Likewise, George Washington, a Macon County freedman, was a wealthy sawmill operator and landowner who later moved to the Oregon Territory and is generally credited with being the founder of Centralia, Washington.

Yet another black entrepreneur who both contributed to and prospered from westward expansion was Hiram Young. A resident of Independence, a place from which many westward-heading wagon trains started, Young owned and operated a huge wagon factory and general blacksmithing business. His reputation was so good and his business so prosperous that he employed a crew of about fifty men, both blacks and whites.

Undoubtedly Missouri's most famous black seamstress was Elizabeth Keckley who saved the earnings from her trade and purchased her freedom in 1855. Later she left her native St. Louis to become the employee and confidante of Mrs. Abraham Lincoln.

The Colored Aristocracy of St. Louis

Nowhere were there more of these individual success stories than in St. Louis. In fact, there emerged in that city during the years preceding the Civil War what Cyprian Clamorgan, a contemporary, called "The Colored Aristocracy." Clamorgan, himself a freedman, claimed in 1858 that free blacks in St. Louis controlled several millions of dollars worth of real and personal property. According to Clamorgan, Mrs. Pilagie Nash owned nearly the whole block in which she lived. Mrs. Sarah Hazlett, a widow, possessed a fortune of $75,000. Samuel Mordecai, with a business at Fourth and Pine Streets, had amassed $100,000. Albert White, a barber who came to St. Louis with $15,000, took his wife to California and returned with an even bigger fortune. William Johnson, a realtor who started with a barber shop in 1840, commanded an estate of $125,000 in 1858. A cattle dealer, Louis Charleville, owned a business worth $60,000. Another wealthy cattle dealer, Antoine Labadie, controlled a business worth $300,000.

This colored aristocracy was made up primarily of mulattoes. Their places of residence were clustered around several streets: Seventh, Rutger, Third between Hazel and Lombard, Fourth and Pine, and Fifteenth near Clark Avenue. As a class, they looked down upon their darker brothers, tended to marry among their own group and thereby maintained as close a connection with the whites as lightness of complexion would allow.

Whether wealthy and successful as were the St. Louis "aristocrats," or struggling as were so many other free blacks, in the long run they prospered in Missouri even under stifling disabilities and strictures. Those courageous blacks proved a living refutation of the black man's "inferiority" and alleged inability to live in a predominantly white society. By building churches and schools, entering into business and putting to use skills learned in slavery, they demonstrated both their ability and their willingness to move into the mainstream of society, if only whites would give them the opportunity.

SUGGESTED READINGS

There has been no book-length study of free blacks in Missouri. Perhaps the best place to begin is with Harrison A. Trexler's book, *Slavery in Missouri, 1804-1865* (Baltimore 1914). Trexler devotes a chapter to "Manumission, Colonization and Emancipation." Trexler's work is best supplemented by several articles by Donnie D. Bellamy: "Free Blacks in Antebellum Missouri, 1820-1960," *Missouri Historical Review*, LXVII (January 1973), pages 198-226, a study which while not definitive certainly points the way for future studies of the Missouri free black community; "The Education of Blacks in Missouri Prior to 1861," *Journal of Negro History*, LIX (April 1974), pages 143-157; and "The Persistency of Colonization in Missouri," *Missouri Historical Review*, LXXII (October 1977), pages 1-24.

The story of freedmen in St. Louis, where the heaviest concentration of free blacks resided, is adequately told by Judy Day and M. James Kedro in "Free Blacks in St. Louis: Antebellum Conditions, Emancipation, and the Post War Era," *Bulletin* (Missouri Historical Society), XXX (January 1974), pages 117-135. The major achievements of Meachum's career are detailed by N. Webster Moore, "John Berry Meachum (1789-1854): St. Louis Pioneer, Black Abolitionist, Educator, and Preacher," *Bulletin* [Missouri Historical Society], XXIX (January 1973), pages 96-103. Likewise, one can gain insight into antebellum free black life in St. Louis by reading Elizabeth Keckley's autobiography, *Behind the Scenes: Thirty Years a Slave and Four in the White House* (New York, 1868). Another contemporary document of great importance is Cyprian Clamorgan, *The Colored Aristocracy of St. Louis,* edited by Lawrence O. Christensen, *Bulletin* [Missouri Historical Society], XXX (October 1974), pages 3-31.

The role that blacks played in buying their own freedom is dealt with by Lorenzo J. Greene in his "Self-Purchase by Negroes in Cole County, Missouri," *Midwest Journal,* I (Winter 1948), pages 83-85. Likewise, the role of religion in the life of antebellum freedmen is touched upon in Gaston Hugh Wamble, "Negroes and Missouri Protestant Churches Before and After the Civil War," *Missouri Historical Review,* LXI (April 1967), pages 321-347. Finally, the participation of Missouri blacks in the westward movement is covered in two works by W. Sherman Savage: "The Negro in the Westward Movement," *Journal of Negro History,* XXV (October 1940), pages 531-539, and *Blacks in the West* (Westport, Connecticut, 1976).

5

The Sable Arm:
Blacks in the Civil War

On April 13, 1861, the Confederates fired on Fort Sumter in Charleston harbor, and on the afternoon of the next day, that Union stronghold fell. The bloodiest civil strife in American history was underway. President Lincoln, unwilling to submit to any compromise, called for seventy-five thousand volunteers to suppress the rebellion. The more realistic Jefferson Davis, president of the newly-formed Confederate States, called for one hundred thousand. Neither total was adequate; by the time the war ended in 1865, the casualty list alone totaled more than one million.

The War Begins: Crucial National Questions

The Border States. The Civil War pitted two vastly different forces against each other. Eleven southern states left the Union—states inferior in number, population, and resources to their northern neighbors who were firmly committed to maintaining the Union. Between these two sides, each patriotically devoted to its own values and way of life, stood the border states, Kentucky, Maryland and Missouri. These states, including Missouri, were essential pawns in the overall war strategy. Without them the South could not win; without them, victory for the North would be delayed or even lost. In 1861, President Lincoln stated that if the border states seceded, the job of preserving the Union would be "too large for us."

Lincoln was especially concerned about Missouri, which he described as the key to the west. Missouri was, of course, a border slave state. Many of its population of nearly 1,200,000 had migrated from the South, so that Missouri had a strong prosouthern minority. With 114,391 slaves and 3,572 free blacks, many of the state's residents felt psychologically tied to the South. Yet the majority of Missourians wanted to see the Union sustained at all costs, although many hoped that slavery would be preserved.

Guerrilla warfare, however, encouraged by Confederate General Sterling Price's forays into the countryside, plagued the state. Killing, burning, and plundering became common events. Kansas Jayhawkers, led by Jim Lane and Colonel Jennison, laid waste the western counties of Missouri. Meanwhile, the distracted and divided state sent its sons into both armies. Thus, while 109,000 Missourians fought for the Stars and Stripes of the Union, 30,000 were fighting under the Stars and Bars of the Confederacy.

Shall the Slaves Be Freed? When the war began in 1861, Lincoln denied any intention to interfere with slavery—to do so would risk losing the crucial border states, tempting them to join the Confederacy. He did realize, however, that something had to be done about slavery. The president tried to persuade border state congressmen to pass legislation paying masters for freeing their slaves. His proposal included a scheme for sending the freedmen out of the country, to Haiti or Liberia. But Lincoln failed to convince these leaders that slaves in their states should be freed.

Lincoln's hand was quickly forced. Just six months after the war began, his commander of the Western Department, John C. Fremont, declared martial law throughout Missouri and on August 30, 1861, issued a proclamation freeing the slaves of anti-Union Missourians. The president reacted quickly and rescinded what he considered to be Fremont's bold and reckless proclamation.

But over the next year political pressure from the Radical wing of Lincoln's own Republican party, as well as the recognition that black soldiers were needed to win the war, meant he had to make a decision. His solution, the famous Emancipation Proclamation, was a stroke of political genius. It freed, as of January 1, 1863, all of the slaves residing in states which were still in rebellion against the Union. The border states were not affected, and the Radicals were

ORDER OF SECESSION

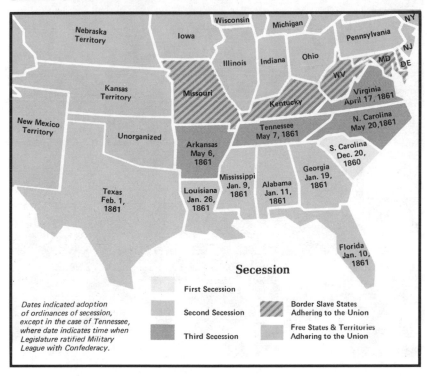

Secession

First Secession

*Dates indicated adoption
of ordinances of secession,
except in the case of Tennessee,
where date indicates time when
Legislature ratified Military
League with Confederacy.*

Second Secession

Border Slave States
Adhering to the Union

Third Secession

Free States & Territories
Adhering to the Union

happy. Lincoln tacked on a provision making slaves eligible for military service.

Shall Black Soldiers Be Used? Thus for a year and half from the war's beginning to the Emancipation Proclamation, Missouri was a slave state loyal to the Union. The first effective challenge to slavery in Missouri came as a result of the debate over whether or not blacks should be enlisted in the Union army. The pressure on Lincoln was intense: slaveholders in the border states like Missouri feared enlisting blacks, while abolitionists, black and white alike, vigorously urged the president to enroll blacks. Perhaps most persuasive of all was the argument of the famous black leader Frederick Douglass, who likened Lincoln's refusal to use blacks to the plight of a man forced to fight with one arm tied behind his back. On July 31, 1863, Lincoln ordered that all available able-bodied blacks between the ages of twenty and forty-five be enrolled and be made part of the armed forces. The decision

Black soldiers during the Civil War. (*State Historical Society of Missouri*)

was momentous because all black volunteers and draftees into the Union army were to be forever free.

The Black Presence in the Union Army. Despite a variety of impediments to black recruitment, more than 180,000 blacks served in the Union cause. They made up about 10 percent of the total Union enlistments. These men are credited with taking part in five hundred military actions, and nearly forty major battles. More than 20 percent of their number gave their lives—almost thirty-seven thousand. In addition, some twenty-nine thousand blacks served in the Union navy; they represented 25 percent of that service's manpower. Seventeen black soldiers and four black sailors were awarded the nation's highest military decoration, the Congressional Medal of Honor.

Although the official figures state that there were 186,017 black troops in the Union army, the exact number will probably never be known because records of black troops were carelessly kept. In order to draw a dead man's pay, white officers often filled the place of a dead black soldier with a new recruit who answered to the same name. Joseph T. Wilson, author of *The Black Phalanx: a History of the Negro Soldiers of the United States in the Wars of 1775-1812, 1861-1865,* and himself a member of both the 2nd Louisiana Native Guard Volunteers and the 54th Massachusetts Volunteers, wrote in 1885 that "if a company on picket or scouting lost ten men, the officer would immediately put ten new men in their places and have them answer to the dead men's names. I learn from very reliable sources that this was done in Virginia, also in Missouri and Tennessee." Wilson concluded that because of this procedure, probably 220,000 black men rather than 180,000 entered the Union army.

Missouri Remains Loyal

Missouri Refuses to Secede. It took two years for the important questions about slavery and black soldiers to be answered on the national level. Meanwhile Missouri had had to deal with these and other questions locally.

In January 1861, Governor Claiborne Jackson asked the Missouri General Assembly to convene a state convention to deal with the question of secession. A special election of delegates was held in February, with 110,000 votes going to candidates who supported the Union and only 30,000 votes going to secessionists. The convention was held in March and was presided over by a southern sympathizer, former Governor Sterling Price. Unionists controlled the proceedings and the convention refused to support secession. However, when Lincoln fixed Missouri's quota of volunteers for the Union army at four thousand men, Governor Jackson refused to comply. Instead, he tried to lead the reluctant state into the Confederacy and set out to raise a rebel militia of fifty thousand men. Jackson was forced to abandon his plan and flee the capital when Union forces under General Nathaniel Lyon entered Jefferson City in mid-1861.

With the governor in exile, and his administration in a shambles, the Unionist forces held another convention in July 1861. They declared all state offices vacant and elected pro-Union conservative Hamilton R. Gamble as their provisional governor. The last serious military threat to the state was a bloody battle at Pea Ridge, Arkansas, on March 6-8, 1862. Union forces won that battle, and thereafter Missouri was steadfastly loyal to the United States.

Recruiting Missouri Blacks. Once the Union decided to use black soldiers, earnest attempts were made to enlist them. In May 1863, Adjutant General Lorenzo Thomas was sent into the Mississippi valley to recruit black soldiers. Later in the fall, his jurisdiction was extended to include Maryland, Tennessee, and Missouri. By that time, Lincoln was convinced that the use of black soldiers was necessary to the salvation of the Union. Accordingly, he wrote Governor Andrew Johnson of Tennessee that "the colored population is the great available and yet unavailed of force for restoring the Union. Fifty thousand armed and drilled black soldiers upon the banks of the Mississippi would end the rebellion at once."[1]

There were drawbacks, however, which discouraged would-be black enlistees, not the least of which was the unequal pay that a member of one of the colored regiments could expect to earn. General Orders No. 163, June 4, 1863, set the pay of black soldiers at ten dollars a month and one ration, three dollars of which was to be used for clothing. This was the wage scale for army laborers, set by the Militia Act of July 17, 1862, and was paid to black combatants and noncombatants alike. By contrast, white volunteers received thirteen dollars a month, three dollars of which was for clothing. The pay scale was finally equalized in June 1864, retroactive to January of that year. Arrears payments to black soldiers for those early months of 1864 were not made until after the war was over.

Closely associated with wages was the matter of bounty. From the outset of hostilities, the federal government paid one hundred dollars bounty to any person volunteering for two years or for the duration of the conflict. Supplementing this were state bounties, ranging from three hundred dollars in Connecticut to five dollars in Wisconsin. County, local, and even private organizations added to the volunteers' incentive. In most instances, blacks saw none of this money. If the slave was drafted, the master received the bounty of one hundred dollars. If the slave volunteered, the master received three hundred dollars, the equivalent of a sort of compensated emancipation. Many people, President Lincoln included, felt that blacks had so much to gain by being taken into the army that they should be willing to join under any circumstances. The muster rolls of various Missouri black companies for 1863-1865 show different amounts under the heading "Entitled to bounty." Sometimes the amount is one hundred dollars; at other times, three hundred. In many cases, no amount is indicated. Not until the summer of June 1864 were black soldiers entitled to a bounty of one hundred dollars.

Missouri Blacks Respond. Lincoln was correct in his assessment— military service was the passport from slavery to freedom. Missouri

John Draine, member of the 67th U. S. Colored
Infantry. *(Lincoln University)*

slaves like blacks in other states enthusiastically embraced the opportunity to join the army. But there were additional incentives. Newspaper articles recruited black soldiers from Boston to St. Louis to fill
the ranks of the prestigious 54th Massachusetts Regiment. Likewise,
when Missouri blacks heard that the 1st Kansas Regiment of Negro
Soldiers had defeated a guerrilla force at Mound Island, Missouri, on
October 27, 1862, their eagerness to join was increased.

The army began recruiting the first black regiment in Missouri in
June 1863 at Schofield Barracks in St. Louis. By June 10, the St. Louis
Tri-Weekly Democrat announced that more than three hundred blacks
had enlisted. The ranks of the First Regiment of Missouri Colored
Infantry were virtually complete by the end of 1863. This unit became
the 62nd U. S. Regiment of Colored Infantry. By January 1864 another
regiment was being organized. According to General Schofield, Com-

mander of the Department of Missouri, the 1st Missouri Infantry of African Descent and the 2nd Infantry of African Descent were among the 4,486 officers and men at Benton Barracks, St. Louis.

During 1864, Grant's Wilderness Campaign and Sherman's march through Georgia accelerated the demand for additional soldiers. Throughout the year Lincoln made repeated calls for more men. Black troops were needed to help fill the quotas assigned Missouri. As a result, 1864 saw the largest recruitment of Missouri blacks. By February 2 of that year, forty-six Assistant Provost Marshals in as many towns had enrolled 3,700 blacks. St. Louis provided 670; Jefferson City, 399; Louisiana, 356; Troy, 343; Macon, 292; Lexington, 272; Tipton, 267; Mexico, 213; Hannibal, 206; Glasgow, 193; Fayette, 172; Sedalia, 169; Marshall, 167; Carrollton, 165; Chillicothe, 105; Columbia, 103. Liberty, Potosi, Ironton, Kingston, St. Charles, Cape Girardeau, Springfield, Pilot Knob, and Washington had at least forty or more soldiers. Howard County reported that six hundred of its nine hundred blacks of military age enlisted in the Union army.

Occasionally, blacks enlisted in the state militia. Generally the Missouri militia was restricted to white men, but at least one independent colored militia company was formed at Hannibal in the fall of 1864. This company had ninety-nine members, captained by C. W. A. Cartlidge. The company was raised for emergency duty to guard prisoners being transported to and from headquarters. It was active for two months. The men were not paid, however, until ten years later.

Not all blacks were volunteers; some, like white men, had to be drafted. On November 14, 1864, 164 men from Boone County were called before the draft board of St. Charles. Since this county had failed to meet its draft quota by eighty-two men, this number was taken from the 164. Of those drafted, twenty-two were black.

Opposition by Whites. Despite the enthusiastic response of blacks to enlistment opportunities, several factors operated to slow down their enrollment in Missouri. Many persons vigorously opposed blacks serving in the armed forces. Slavemasters were particularly hostile, since enlistment of the slave was equal to a writ of emancipation. T. M. Allen of Boone County summed up this sentiment in a letter dated February 12, 1864, to his representative in Washington, James S. Rollins:

> I think Missouri has been badly treated by the Administration. No State in the Union has made the same sacrifices for peace as we have. . . .Was it just to issue an order to enlist the slaves of Union men as well as Rebels? Was not this virtually issuing an edict emancipating forthwith our Negroes?

Conservative officials also sought to block the recruiting of slaves, for they felt that such recruitment would incite the bondsmen to rebellion. Judges of circuit courts charged grand juries in Marion County and in western parts of the state to invoke Article I of the *Revised Missouri Statutes*, which provided the death penalty for anyone convicted of "inciting rebellion or insurrection among slaves, Mulattoes, or free Negroes."

Guerrillas, by terrorizing blacks, also acted to retard recruiting. The famous guerrilla leader William Quantrill threatened death to anyone answering Lincoln's proclamation for volunteers. He and other leaders of bushwhacking bands often frightened blacks away from recruiting stations. Sometimes terrorism resulted in murder. The official records and newspapers report many cases of blacks being killed by guerrilla bands. Several hangings and shootings of blacks in the fall of 1863 were capped by what contemporary sources described as a "massacre" of three blacks in Boone County on November 18, 1863. According to county Provost Marshal C. F. Russell, these killings were intended as a warning for all blacks to leave the county in ten days or be killed by raiders.

Missouri Blacks at War

Regiments. In all, seven Negro regiments were enrolled in Missouri. The official figures place the total number of men at 8,400 with 665 serving as substitutes for whites who had been drafted. But even this figure does not accurately reflect the number of black Missourians actually sent to the Union army. Many Missouri blacks served in out-of-state regiments. This was especially true in the 1st Iowa Regiment of African Descent and the 1st and 2nd Regiments of Kansas Colored Volunteers. Others enlisted in Illinois, Ohio, and even Massachusetts units. Black soldiers made up almost one-twelfth the total number of troops contributed by Missouri to the Union army. Missouri ranked fifth in the number of black troops furnished, behind Louisiana with 24,052, Kentucky with 23,703, Tennessee with 20,133, and Mississippi with 17,869. Of the total 186,017 blacks in the service of the Union, Missouri contributed 4.4 percent.

In Battle and Service. Black Missourians saw action in a number of contests. Members of the 18th Regiment fought at the Battle of Nashville and pursued General Hood to the Tennessee River in 1865. The 62nd saw action in Texas, including a skirmish at White's Ranch, the last battle of the war. The 67th spent most of its time in Louisiana and participated in a battle at Mt. Pleasant Landing in May 1864. The 68th helped to make up the force that assaulted and captured Ft. Blakely, Alabama, in April 1865. The 65th performed mostly fatigue duty in the unhealthy Louisiana swamps. Sickness claimed the lives of an incredible number of men from its ranks: six officers and 749 enlisted men.

Blacks performed other valuable services for the Union army besides fighting. They acted as informants and spies, pointing out locations of bushwhackers and guerrillas. Black men worked as teamsters, cooks, builders of breastworks, and in other noncombat capacities. Many black women also served as nurses.

Discrimination followed black soldiers into the services. Often they were given inferior weapons and supplies. They usually received inadequate medical care. At first, they were likely to be killed by the Confederates if they were captured, until Lincoln and Grant threatened to treat captured rebels in a similar manner.

The conclusion is inescapable that blacks played a vital role in the Union victory. Lincoln himself acknowledged the importance of their role. A skeptic at first about the worth of the black soldier, Lincoln later became enthusiastic in describing his contribution. The president openly declared that the nation could not be saved without this sable arm.

The Consequences of the War

Self-Esteem and Dignity. Psychologically, the Civil War had a tremendous effect upon the black soldier. Blacks generally, and soldiers in particular, identified the Civil War as their own American Revolution. The war transformed and regenerated them. The black soldier went into the army as a despised and degraded chattel, mere property, having no name except the one given him by his master. He came to the recruiting station as "George," "Andy," or "Primus." He came out a man, as "George Washington," "Andrew Jackson," or "Primus Davis." Putting on the uniform of the United States enhanced his self-esteem and his dignity. It gave him a sense of identity with the struggle for human freedom, and fired him with the conviction that he was sharing in a great humanitarian crusade that went beyond his own experiences. Sergeant Prince Rivers, a black soldier of the 1st South Carolina Volunteers, spoke for black soldiers everywhere when he summed up what the war meant to him:

> Now we sogers are men—men de first time in our lives. Now we can look our old masters in de face. They used to sell and ship us, and we did not dare say one word. Now we ain't afraid, if they meet us, to run the bayonet through them.[2]

Freed Negroes, after Emancipation Proclamation, 1863. *(State Historical Society of Missouri)*

Freedom. As the events of the Civil War unfolded during more than four years of bloody strife, black people in Missouri and elsewhere prepared for what they believed would soon be the day of freedom. The war uprooted many of them. Wartime chaos in Missouri prompted many masters to transport their slaves to Arkansas or even Texas in an attempt to salvage something from their investment. Thousands of slaves simply abandoned their masters, particularly if there were Union troops in the immediate vicinity. Many carried with them as many of the master's possessions as they could handle—"spiling the Egyptians," they called it. Some wandered to towns such as Columbia, Jefferson City, or St. Louis. Others sought the more secure borders of free states such as Kansas, Illinois, Iowa, or Michigan. It has been estimated that of the more than one hundred thousand slaves in Missouri in 1860, only eighty-five thousand were still in bondage in 1862 and not more than twenty-two thousand in 1864. The precariousness of slave property was reflected in a drastic drop in price, from approximately thirteen hundred dollars in 1860 to one hundred dollars in 1864.

Some idea of what happened in one town can be gleaned from a report by Sheriff Bruns of Cole County in January 1865. Sheriff Bruns was asked by local officials to take a census of the county. He discovered that there were 565 blacks in Jefferson City, a marked increase over the 333 of 1860. Moreover, the sheriff indicated, despite the fact that only three of the black residents were described as free, all of them were virtually so, "belonging either to the class called contrabands, or to the number whose masters had ceased to make any effort to control them."

For many black soldiers, the greatest boost they had gotten out of the freedom struggle had been that they had proved their manhood. Or, as one black soldier put it:

> We can remember, when we fust enlisted, it was hardly safe for we to pass by de camps to Beaufort and back, lest we went in a mob and carried side arms. But we whipped down all dat—not by going into de white camps for whip um; we didn't tote our bayonets for whip um; but we lived it down by our naturally manhood; and now de white sojers take us by de hand and say Broder Sojer. Dats what dis regiment did for de Epiopian race.
>
> If we hadn't become sojers, all might have gone back as it was before; our freedom might have slipped through de two houses of Congress and President Linkum's four years might have passed by and notin' been done for us. But now tings can neber go back, because we have showed our energy and our courage and our naturally manhood.[3]

Education. As the war drew to a close, many black and white leaders, aware that slavery was a dying institution, tried to arrange educational opportunities for slaves and free blacks alike. They viewed education as the single most important key to black movement into the mainstream of American life. Black and white educational efforts on behalf of blacks were so large in St. Louis that a black Board of Education was established. The unofficial board had charge of four schools with four hundred students. By 1865, the system had eight teachers and six hundred pupils.

In 1865, the Western Sanitary Commission, a white benevolent association, operated a high school in St. Louis for about fifty blacks in the basement of a local church. The commission also organized classes for black soldiers at Benton Barracks. The instruction, mostly in reading and writing, continued in the black regiments. The officers of the black outfits, many of them college-trained, often taught the former slaves around the campfires.

The federally-sponsored Freedmen's Bureau was also effective in offering financial support for local black education near the end of the war. During the war years, however, the most important single force supporting black education was probably the American Missionary Association. In the late 1850s, the AMA, as it was known, had unsuccessfully tried to convert the Missouri slaveholder to the abolitionist gospel. Forcefully and violently driven out of Missouri at the start of the Civil War, the AMA returned in 1862. This time the main thrust of the organization was to provide the former slaves with a Christian education.

Despite black eagerness to receive education, the AMA encountered constant opposition to its efforts. In 1863, an AMA school that served sixty black pupils in St. Louis was burned by a group of whites. The school had been open for only three days. By 1865, AMA agents were located in several Missouri communities, including Jefferson City, Warrensburg, Holt County, Kansas City, and Carondelet. The society's teachers, many of whom were women, were often intimidated and threatened with physical violence. In Carondelet, the AMA school was closed after only nine weeks because the female teacher could no longer secure living quarters in the unfriendly white community. Alma Baker later reopened this school, but endured much abuse for boarding with a black family. The grateful black community paid her rent out of their meager resources. In Jefferson City, AMA agent, Mrs. L. A. Montague, was labeled the "nigger teacher." She witnessed the destruction of schoolbooks and furniture by local whites. Her black students were stoned on the way to school. However, several white citizens of Jefferson City encouraged Mrs. Montague to continue her work and stand her ground. Moral and financial support for these efforts came from the black community. In Carondelet, Warrensburg, Jefferson City, St. Louis, and other localities, blacks raised money for teachers' board, paid rent on school buildings, and, insofar as they were able, paid teachers' salaries.

A New Day. Throughout the former slave states, blacks believed a new day had dawned. The end of the war and of slavery had turned their world upside down. They were uncertain about what it all meant, and what the future held for them. Signs of optimism abounded—a new status as freedmen, a new sense of belonging and worth, new opportunities in education—all proof that whatever lay ahead was better than what had gone before.

NOTES

1. Quoted in V. Jacques Voegeli, Free But Not Equal: The Midwest and the Negro During the Civil War (Chicago, 1967), page 105.

2. Leon Litwack, Been in the Storm So Long: The Aftermath of Slavery (New York, 1979), page 64.

3. Quoted in the introduction to Thomas Wentworth Higginson, Army Life in a Black Regiment (New York, 1962), pages 19-20.

SUGGESTED READINGS

The best general treatment of blacks in the Civil War is Benjamin Quarles, *The Negro in the Civil War* (Boston, 1953). Lincoln's goals in issuing the Emancipation Proclamation are the subject of John Hope Franklin, *The Emancipation Proclamation* (Garden City, N.Y., 1963). Dudley T. Cornish, *The Sable Arm: Negro Troops in the Union Army 1861-1865* (New York, 1956) is well done as is James M. McPherson, *The Negroes' Civil War* (New York, 1965), and his *The Struggle for Equality* (Princeton, 1964). At the state level, there is John W. Blassingame, "The Recruitment of Negro Troops in Missouri During the Civil War," *Missouri Historical Review,* LVIII (April 1964), pages 326-338.

The politics of Missouri are thoroughly treated in William E. Parrish, *The Turbulent Partnership: Missouri and the Union 1861-1865* (Columbia, 1963). Guerrilla warfare in Missouri is dealt with in Richard S. Brownlee, *Gray Ghosts of the Confederacy: Guerrilla Warfare in the West, 1861-1865* (Baton Rouge, 1958). Some of the efforts in support of black education are covered by Joe M. Richardson, "The American Missionary Association and Black Education in Civil War Missouri," *Missouri Historical Review,* LXIX (July 1975), pages 433-448.

6

Forty Acres and a Mule:
Reconstruction in Missouri
1865-1877

he Civil War drastically altered black life in America. Former slaves were thrust into a fundamentally new social, political, and economic position. Innumerable obstacles presented themselves as the freedmen sought to adjust to a new way of living for which slavery had ill-prepared them. Without money, property, or education, they tried to move into the mainstream of a highly competitive, literate, capitalistic society.

Emancipation: The Promise and the Reality

The Joy of Freedom. The freedmen's initial response to the ending of slavery was influenced very little by the fear of burdens that lay ahead. Missouri's slaves were freed on January 11, 1865, an action that was pushed through a state convention dominated by members of the Radical Unionist party. Thus Missouri blacks gained their freedom eleven months before the ratification of the Thirteenth Amendment to the United States Constitution ended the institution of slavery nationally. Blacks throughout the state rejoiced. On Sunday, January 14, thousands took to the streets of St. Louis, Jefferson City, and other communities with flags and banners proclaiming their joy at finally having achieved their most sought-after dream. Others celebrated

more privately, often thanking God for deliverance from their bondage.
Such was the case of a black servant who greeted the news of freedom
as follows:

> I jump up an' scream, "Glory, glory, hallelujah to Jesus! I's free!
> Glory to God, you come down an' free us; no big man could do it."
> An' I got sort o' scared, afeared somebody hear me, an' I takes
> another good look an' fall on de groun', an' roll over, an' kiss
> de groun' fo' de Lord's sake, I's so full a' praise to Masser Jesus.
> He do all dis great work. De soul buyers can neber take my two
> chillen lef' me; no, neber can take 'em from me no mo'.[1]

Blacks would soon realize, however, that because slavery had largely
confined them to performing menial or farm laborer tasks, they were
now just additional unskilled workers thrown upon an already overcrowded job market.

The Reality of Racism. An even more serious problem than the lack of
preparation and training was the persistence of antiblack sentiment
in the state. Slavery died hard in Missouri and the slave code mentality
lived on for many years after the Civil War. Conservative counties, like
the "Kingdom of Callaway," regarded emancipation with hatred. The
last year of the war in Missouri saw a sharp increase in guerrilla activity, a violent response to the frustration that southern sympathizers
felt. Often the guerrillas vented their wrath upon innocent freedmen
who had become a symbol of all that the bushwhackers detested.

One of the more infamous of the lawless bandits who roamed the
state was Jim Jackson, who led his gang into Boone County in mid-
February of 1865 and lynched one of Dr. John Jacobs' black hired
hands. This was a warning both to freedmen who sought work and
whites who hired them. Referring to racial violence, General Clinton
B. Fisk wrote in March 1865, the following account of what he had
seen in his travels throughout the state:

> Slavery dies hard. I hear its expiring agonies and witness its
> contortions in death in every quarter of my district. In Boone,
> Howard, Randolph, and Callaway the emancipation ordinance
> has caused disruption of society equal to anything I saw in Ar-
> kansas or Mississippi in the year 1863. I blush for my race when I
> discover the wicked barbarity of the late masters and mistresses of
> the recently freed persons of the counties heretofore named. I
> have no doubt but that the monster, Jim Jackson, is instigated by
> the late slave owners to hang or shoot every negro he can find
> absent from the old plantations. Some few have driven their black
> people away from them with nothing to eat or scarcely to wear.
> The consequence is, between Jim Jackson and his colaborers
> [sic] among the first families, the poor blacks are rapidly concen-
> trating in the towns and especially at garrisoned places. My

hands and heart are full. I am finding homes for them in Northwest Missouri, Kansas, Illinois, and Iowa. There is much sickness
and suffering among them; many need help. . . .[2]

As General Fisk's comments suggest, many blacks responded to
oppression in Missouri by fleeing the state as soon as they gained their
freedom. In fact, there were fewer blacks in the state in 1870 than there
had been ten years before, a decline from 118,503 to 118,071. Some
of those who stayed tried to find jobs with their former masters or
other whites. Often their pay was only room and board. By 1870, more
than two-thirds of the black males employed in the state were still
working as farm laborers.

Harassment. Even if blacks were able to find employment, they faced
other burdens. Although Missouri escaped much of the segregation
legislation that would later dominate the South, there were informal
codes of behavior designed to ensure that blacks knew their place.
For example, streetcar companies in St. Louis prohibited blacks from
riding inside their cars. In 1867, Caroline Williams, a black woman,
pregnant and holding a baby, tried to board a car only to be shoved into
the street by the conductor. She and her husband sued the company.
They won their suit, but were awarded damages of only one cent.
Nevertheless a principle of law had been established which effectively
ended the practice of keeping blacks out of streetcars.

Efforts by blacks to obtain education often met with opposition in
the form of arson. In 1866, a school for blacks at Linneus in northwest
Missouri was set afire by whites; the fire was extinguished before
major damage was done. In January 1867, white youths burned a new
school for blacks in Fulton, and in the same year a drunken band of
whites fired pistols into a black Christmas Eve congregation at St.
Paul's Church in St. Louis County. They killed one person and
wounded another. Similar acts of violence occurred in other parts of
the state.

Moving Into the Mainstream

National Leadership. What was being done to help blacks adjust to
freedom, in the face of white racism and violence? Nationally, the
Radical Republicans were trying to enact legislation that would at
least ensure blacks equal protection before the law and the right to
vote. While they never provided the legendary "forty acres and a mule"
that many blacks were led to believe would be forthcoming, the Radicals did advance the black cause. Under the congressional leadership
of men such as Charles Sumner and Thaddeus Stevens, they pushed

through three important amendments to the constitution. The Thirteenth Amendment, ratified in 1865, abolished slavery forever. The Fourteenth Amendment (1868) guaranteed blacks equal protection of the laws and all civil liberties enjoyed by white persons. The Fifteenth Amendment (1870) granted the freedmen the coveted right to vote.

Another way the federal government hoped to assist the freedmen was by encouraging them to save their money in order to secure a stronger economic position in the social order. As a result, it created in 1865 the National Freedmen's Savings and Trust Company, better known as the Freedmen's Bank. In 1868, a St. Louis branch was established under the presidency of the Rev. W. P. Brooks, who served for the entire six years of the bank's life. Born a slave in Virginia in 1826, Brooks moved to Missouri in 1842, purchased his freedom in 1846 for one thousand dollars, and became actively involved in the Underground Railroad and black education. He conducted a wood and coal business in St. Louis from 1855 to 1865. In 1865, he sold his business for three thousand dollars after deciding that he wanted to spend more time in the ministry. The St. Louis Freedmen's Savings and Trust Company was a marginal operation at best, largely because black Missourians had so little money to save. It later fell victim to the financial crisis that swept the country during the Panic of 1873.

The national Radicals also counted heavily on private philanthropy to help blacks. The Radicals established the Freedmen's Bureau, a national organization formed to help both whites and blacks adjust to the new situation. Freedmen's Bureau agents came to Missouri in the spring of 1865. They started setting up schools for blacks, seeing to it that all slave couples were legally "remarried" in accordance with state law, providing the destitute with food, medicine, clothing, and shelter, and arranging labor contracts with farmers. More than one thousand Missouri blacks received some form of direct aid from the Freedmen's Bureau in the immediate postwar period.

Another white philanthropic organization serving the freedmen was the Western Sanitary Commission established in 1861. The commission was especially active in the St. Louis area, where it organized four elementary schools and one high school. The commission also set up a Freedmen's Orphans' Home for abandoned children of slaves.

Radical Republicans and the Missouri Constitution. White assistance came from local sources as well, primarily from Radical Republicans. Although many Missouri Radicals who favored emancipation also endorsed the removal of freedmen from the state, the constitution which they drew up in 1865 was a relatively progressive document. Emancipation was quickly granted, but the exact nature of rights which the freed blacks were to enjoy caused much more difficulty. The issues centered on the three questions of whether blacks should be allowed to testify against whites in court cases, to vote and to hold office, and to receive educational opportunities at the state's expense.

The first question was resolved by deciding that no person could be denied the right to testify because of his or her race. The Radicals then cleared the way for state-established black schools by including a provision in the constitution stating that the General Assembly could establish schools "for children of African descent." Funds for all public schools were to be appropriated "in proportion to the number of children without regard to color."

However, the Radicals moved more cautiously on the suffrage issue. The vast majority of Missourians remained hesitant about whether to allow blacks the right to vote. Even the Radical leader, Charles Drake, was skeptical about including a black suffrage plank in the constitution, fearing that it would cause the entire document to be rejected by Missouri voters. Consequently, the privileges of voting and office-holding were limited to qualified white males.

Equal Rights and Black Activism

The Missouri Equal Rights League. Because the convention which drafted the new state constitution soundly rejected the inclusion of blacks' right to vote and hold office, blacks in Missouri felt they lacked an essential freedom. The result was the organization of Missouri's first black political activist movement—the Missouri Equal Rights League. The organizational meeting of the League in October 1865, was held at a church on the corner of Green and Eighth Streets in St. Louis. It was dominated by black St. Louis religious leaders, although freedmen from other parts of the state were present.

The blacks gathered in St. Louis called attention to their plight as freedmen who lacked the rights and privileges of the elective franchise, and charged that such a condition was little better than the oppression they had suffered under slave masters. They pointed out that they too had borne arms in defense of the Union and stated that their future safety and prosperity would be best ensured by the state's declaring all people, regardless of color, equal before the law.

Before adjourning, League members chose a seven-man executive committee to work toward the achievement of this goal. The committee members were H. McGee, Col. F. Robinson, Moses Dickson, J. Bowman, Samuel Helms, Dr. G. Downing, and George Wedley. Specifically, the committee was charged with the responsibility of providing for a series of mass meetings throughout the state, procuring

black speakers, and preparing an address on the plight of black people
to the citizens of Missouri.

The Rev. Moses Dickson, prominent black St. Louisan, was probably the best known of these men. His involvement with the Equal
Rights League represented the continuation of a struggle for black
freedom that he had begun long before. After traveling through the
South from 1840-43, observing the plight of slaves, the Rev. Dickson
recruited twelve men and formed a group called the Knights of
Liberty. This group aimed to enlist and arm southern slaves for a
general rebellion. At one point, the Knights claimed to have forty-seven
thousand members. The group set the year 1856 as the time for revolution. As the year approached, however, and the antislavery struggle
increased in intensity, Dickson counseled his followers to wait for what
he felt certain would be a civil war. When the war came in April 1861,
and after black troops were authorized, Dickson and many of his
followers took up arms in the Union cause. Later, a fraternal organization known as the International Order of Twelve, Knights of Tabor,
was founded to continue the struggle for equality. This organization
still exists today.

Taking the Black Case to Missourians. Two weeks after the executive
committee was appointed, a twenty-seven thousand word *Address to
the Friends of Equal Rights* appeared in local newspapers and as a
pamphlet. It was an elaborate expression of the concerns and aspirations that had been voiced at the October organizational meeting.
The major plea was for the right to vote. The petitioners reminded
their readers that they were citizens of the state and nation and that
their toil had enriched both. They also recalled that nine thousand
black soldiers had "bared their breasts to the remorseless storm of
treason, and by hundreds went down to death in the conflict while the
franchised rebel. . .the. . .bitterest enemy of our right to suffrage, remained. . .at home, safe and fattened on the fruits of our sacrifice, toil
and blood." The *Address* warned that its readers should take seriously
the plea of black Missourians. Finally, they emphasized that the question of what to do with black people would become the greatest issue
before the republic.

The committee hired John M. Langston of Ohio, a well-known
black orator and lawyer, to tour the state in support of its petition.
Langston began his journey by delivering a talk in St. Louis in November 1865. He followed that speech with trips to Hannibal, Macon,
Chillicothe, St. Joseph, Kansas City, Sedalia, and Jefferson City.
Everywhere he went the message was the same: he pleaded with members of both races for black suffrage and for black access to education.

Langston was not the only black spokesman touring the state. Another was James Milton Turner, who was only twenty-six years old when the Civil War ended. Turner was one of the most important black leaders in post-Civil War Missouri. He was born a slave in 1839. His father, who worked as a horse doctor, was able to purchase the family's freedom when Milton was three years old. Educated in St. Louis schools and at Oberlin College in Ohio, Turner was a fiery orator who emerged as secretary of the Missouri Equal Rights League in 1865. Throughout that winter he traveled around the state, especially the southeastern part, advocating education and the ballot for blacks. Turner encountered his strongest opposition in Southeast Missouri, a region that had remained strongly sympathetic to the rebel cause. On one occasion he was forced "to escape for his life at midnight, barefooted in the snow, leaving his shoes behind him."

The executive committee also circulated a petition throughout the state, imploring the legislature to provide suitable schools for black children. It also sought an amendment to the constitution that would remove the word "white," and, in so doing, would guarantee the legal equality of all the state's citizens. The petition gained the signatures of four thousand blacks and whites. It was then turned over to the Honorable Enos Clarke, representative from St. Louis, to present to the legislature. Despite Clarke's strong endorsement of the petition, the legislature refused to act favorably upon it. In fact, the result of all the activism in Missouri was disappointing. Success came only in 1870 when the Fifteenth Amendment to the national constitution guaranteed the right to vote without regard to "race, color, or previous condition of servitude."

The Black Emphasis on Education

The black citizens who made up the Equal Rights League had known that the fight to secure full political and civil rights was not going to be easy. Accordingly they had placed great emphasis on education, to advance the progress of blacks and to refute arguments against blacks' voting which were offered by white opponents. They realized that many freedmen were unprepared for participatory democracy. The executive committee, in its *Address*, emphasized that "we mean to make our freedom *practical*," adding that it saw education as the chief means by which that could be done. Convinced that the responsibilities of citizenship could be best fulfilled by an educated citizenry, the league sought to establish schools for the freedmen wherever possible.

James Milton Turner and Black Education. James Milton Turner, the

Equal Rights League secretary, was the most active and effective
black advocate of education for the former slaves. He taught in two
of the earliest black public schools in the state, at Kansas City and
Boonville. In 1869, Turner was appointed an agent of the American
Missionary Association with the major responsibility of traveling
around the state setting up black schools. During the same year he
received a similar appointment from the Freedmen's Bureau and from
the Radical State Superintendent of Public Schools, T. A. Parker. When
Turner submitted his report to the Freedmen's Bureau in early 1870,
he revealed that he had traveled "between eight and ten thousand
miles." His efforts, he stated, had assured black children that approximately eight thousand dollars of public funds annually would be applied toward their education. In addition, he was instrumental in
erecting at least seven new school buildings and opening thirty-
two schools across the state.

Turner's task was not easy. One of the biggest obstacles he faced,
he wrote, was that "in such sections where the largest number of
colored people are found there is a preponderance of disloyal and
former slave holding peoples, who in most cases are opposed to the
establishment of these [black] schools." Another problem was to find
competent black teachers, since many Missourians were opposed
to white persons teaching black students. Discrimination in salaries
further complicated the issue. As late as 1873, male teachers of black
pupils received only $46.70 a month, while a male teacher in a white
school could expect $82.42. Female teachers in white schools could
expect only $50; in black schools, $46.64.

Black Soldiers Take the Initiative. The need for black teachers did not
go unnoticed by government officials in Jefferson City. State Superintendent of Schools T. A. Parker had written of the desperate need for
black teachers in his annual report of 1869. Parker suggested that the
need could be met by providing state support for newly-established
Lincoln Institute in Jefferson City.

The idea of the institute had originated with the black Missourians
who served in the 62nd United States Colored Infantry. As Lieutenant
Richard B. Foster, a white officer of that regiment, recounted the story,
a number of soldiers were told in January 1866 that they would soon
be sent home. They were happy at the thought of returning home,
and many felt satisfied that they had at least learned the basics of
reading and writing while in the service. Nevertheless, there was
great anxiety among them that what little knowledge they had gained
would be lost if they were not able to go to school back home.

The soldiers began raising money for a school back in Missouri.

Logan Bennett, member of the 65th Infantry.
(Lincoln University)

Money quickly poured in. The lieutenants gave fifty dollars each and
officers of higher rank, one hundred dollars, while enlisted men gave
what they could afford. Meanwhile, Foster was appointed traveling
agent for the soldiers and sent to ask the men of the 65th Infantry, many
of them black Missourians, for additional contributions. The serious-
ness of the commitment these black soldiers felt toward education
is exemplified by Private Samuel Sexton of the 65th, who gave one
hundred dollars, although his annual salary totaled only $156.

Lincoln Institute. The total collected from the 62nd was $5,000.10;
more than $1300 was collected from the 65th. Lieutenant Foster was
designated as the agent to carry the money raised to Missouri and to
set up a school there for freedmen. He was a logical choice, for his

Richard Baxter Foster, first principal of Lincoln
Institute. *(Lincoln University)*

abolitionist and humanitarian credentials were impeccable. Foster was
born and raised in Hanover, New Hampshire, graduated from Dart-
mouth College, and well-steeped in the Congregationalist tradition.
He had taught school in Illinois and Indiana prior to the Civil War.
Foster also demonstrated his abolitionist sentiments as early as 1856
by assisting John Brown in a raid upon Fort Titus, Kansas. In 1862
he entered the service of the Union army as a private in the 1st Ne-
braska Regiment. When President Lincoln authorized the formation
of black regiments, Foster volunteered to join the 62nd United States
Colored Infantry.

Foster took the money and the trust of the black soldiers and
headed for Missouri. Upon his arrival there in the summer of 1866, he
was beset by problems. He made an unsuccessful attempt to establish a
school in St. Louis before he moved west to Jefferson City, only to
encounter additional difficulties. His plight is best summed up by his

James Milton Turner. *(Lincoln University)*

efforts to find a place to house the school. "I applied to the colored
Methodist Church for their house," he wrote in 1871, ". . .but the minister refused, alleging as a reason that the teacher would be white."
"I applied to the white Methodist Church," he continued, ". . .but the
minister refused, alleging as a reason that the scholars would be black."

Foster had to settle for an old log cabin on the outskirts of Jefferson City, at a place called Hobo Hill. The building had previously
been used as a white school, but had since been declared unfit for
human occupancy. He later gave this account of the school's opening:

> The rain is pouring in torrents. As I approached the schoolhouse,
> I am stopped by a creek, the bridge over which has been swept
> away—usually fordable, but now impassable by reason of the
> flood. A half hour's detour, and the scrambling of several fences
> brings me to the sanctuary of learning. What a sanctuary! The
> rains pour through the roof scarcely less than outside. I could
> throw a dog through the side in twenty places. There is no sign

HISTORICAL SKETCH

OF

Lincoln Institute,

JEFFERSON CITY, MISSOURI.

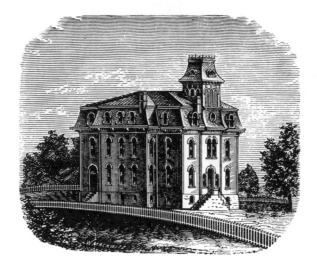

BY

PROF. R. B. FOSTER.

AND SPEECH OF

COL. DAVID BRANSON,

Upon the Dedication of the New Building,

JULY 4th, 1871.

Lincoln Institute, 1871. *(Lincoln University)*

of a window, bench, desk, chair, or table. In this temple of the muses I meet two pupils. On the next day the same scene is repeated. The third day the rain has ceased, the creek has become fordable, and seventeen pupils are enrolled: and for more than six weeks, new names are added to the register every day.[3]

Foster named the school Lincoln Institute. The school struggled along, barely making ends meet, until 1870, when the Radicals' self-interest meshed with black aspirations. James Milton Turner, whose activities on behalf of black education had made him a well-known leader throughout the state, called for a convention of blacks to meet in Jefferson City in January 1870 to petition the legislature for support of Lincoln Institute as a training school for black teachers.

Radical Republicans Seek the Black Vote

The Right to Vote and New Political Realities. The Radicals were in trouble in Missouri by 1869-1870. They were still in control of state government, but that was largely because they continued to deny the vote to former "rebels." There was growing sentiment within the party to restore the franchise to these people, a position that Stalwart Radicals fought against. Congress passed the Fifteenth Amendment on February 26, 1869, and sent it to the states for ratification (achieved in 1870). Many Radicals reasoned that they could neutralize any "rebel" threat by wooing the soon-to-be enfranchised blacks. Their motives were utilitarian and shortsighted. Their support of black causes reflected more the instability of Missouri politics than a genuine expression of concern for black people.

Vote and education (handwritten margin note)

The Radicals' strategy was to identify and latch on to a black leader who they believed could deliver black votes. The man they turned to was James Milton Turner. Turner aspired to become United States Minister to Liberia and in mid-1869 Radicals from Governor Joseph W. McClurg on down the ranks endorsed his candidacy. When Turner convened the January 1870 gathering of black leaders in Jefferson City, the Radicals quickly came to his aid. In February they passed a law granting five thousand dollars annually to Lincoln Institute on the condition that the institute trustees first agree to convert the school into a facility for the training of black public school teachers. On March 10, 1870, the Radicals opened the Hall of Representatives to Lincoln Principal Richard B. Foster and his students for a public recitation. The gathering was designed to attract contributions to the institute. Governor McClurg and other highly-placed Radical officials set the stage for the proceedings by giving one hundred dollars each.

Radical support for Lincoln Institute did not guarantee a warm reception for black students in Jefferson City. Indeed, in 1874 several institute students were turned away from a recital by a Jefferson City author because they were black. Such overt racial discrimination prompted black instructor Lizzie Lindsay to write an eloquent but futile protest:

> These were students thirsting for knowledge, and hearing that Mrs. Siddons' readings were worth attending, they went for the purpose of gaining instruction, yet were subjected to insult merely on account of their color.

> The cry is heard from the Lakes to the Gulf, from the Orient to the Occident, educate the colored people: and how are they to be educated advantageously if colored teachers, students and persons of culture are insulted and outraged by those who *consider* themselves their superiors?

The endorsement of the ballot and education for the freedmen by Radical Republicans further convinced Turner and other blacks that the Radicals were their real benefactors. Subsequently, twenty thousand blacks voted the Radical ticket in 1870. Unfortunately, the continued division within Radical ranks in Missouri over rebel reenfranchisement split the party into Stalwart Radical and Liberal factions. Consequently, a coalition of dissident Liberals and Democrats ousted the Radicals from power in Missouri in 1870. Nationally, the Radicals still held some sway, and President Grant appointed Turner to his eagerly-sought Liberian ministership. Turner held that position from 1871 to 1878, making him only the second black person in the history of the country to become a diplomat.

Foundations for the Future. Turner was the exception, not the rule, however. Most blacks continued to work at relatively low-paying, unskilled jobs. Radical Reconstruction had given them the right to vote and a public commitment to black education. These would be the major vehicles that blacks would use for the next one hundred years in traveling down the narrow and treacherous path in search of full equality.

NOTES

1. Quoted in Laura Haviland, *A Woman's Life-Work: Labors and Experiences of Laura S. Haviland* (Cincinnati, 1882), page 415.

2. Quoted in William E. Parrish, *Missouri Under Radical Rule, 1865-1870* (Columbia, 1965), page 107.

3. Antonio F. Holland and Gary R. Kremer, eds., "Some Aspects of Black Education in Reconstruction Missouri: An Address by Richard B. Foster," *Missouri Historical Review*, LXX (January 1976), page 189.

SUGGESTED READINGS

Any discussion of black life in Reconstruction Missouri must begin with two books by William E. Parrish: *Missouri Under Radical Rule, 1865-1870* (Columbia, 1965), and *A History of Missouri 1860 to 1875*, vol. III of *A History of Missouri*, the Missouri sesquicentennial edition (edited by William E. Parrish, Columbia, 1973). Parrish devotes chapters in each of these books to blacks in the immediate postwar period.

Black education during this period is the subject of Antonio F. Holland and Gary R. Kremer, "Some Aspects of Black Education in Reconstruction Missouri: An Address by Richard B. Foster," *Missouri Historical Review*, LXX (January 1976), pages 184-198. Other articles on black education include W. Sherman Savage, "The Legal Provisions for Negro Schools in Missouri from 1865 to 1890," *Journal of Negro History*, XVI (July 1931), pages 300-321, and Henry S. Williams, "The Development of the Negro Public School System in Missouri," *Journal of Negro History*, V (April 1920), pages 137-165. The story of the founding of Lincoln Institute is told in Savage, *The History of Lincoln University* (Jefferson City, 1939).

The career of prominent black politician James Milton Turner has been the subject of several articles. Gary R. Kremer, "Background to Apostasy: James Milton Turner and the Republican Party, *Missouri Historical Review*, LXXI (October 1976), pages 59-75, details Turner's involvement with the Radicals. Articles covering Turner more generally include the following: Irving Dilliard, "James Milton Turner: A Little Known Benefactor of His People," *Journal of Negro History*, XIX (October 1934), pages 372-411; N. Webster Moore, "James Milton Turner, Diplomat, Educator, and Defender of Rights, 1840-1915," *Bulletin* [Missouri Historical Society], XXVII (April 1971), pages 194-201; Lawrence O. Christensen, "J. Milton Turner: An Appraisal," *Missouri Historical Review*, LXX (October 1975), pages 1-19.

The role of the Freedmen's Bureau in Missouri is covered by W. A. Low, "The Freedmen's Bureau in the Border States," in Richard O. Curry, ed., *Radicalism, Racism, and Party Realignment: the Border States During Reconstruction* (Baltimore, 1969).

7

Separate and Unequal
Reconstruction to World War 1

Although there were disappointments for freedmen during the first decade after emancipation, black people remained generally optimistic during those years. Radical concessions to their cause, both nationally and locally, nourished the dream that equality for all was attainable. There were disturbing trends in the former slave states, however. More and more old-line southern Democrats were rising to positions of power. These Bourbons, as they were called, promised to "redeem" the South from northern, pro-black control. The process was capped in 1877 by the famous compromise that brought President Rutherford B. Hayes to the White House. Hayes narrowly defeated the Democratic challenger, Samuel J. Tilden, in an election that was ultimately decided by a congressionally-appointed commission. Hayes won the contest only after agreeing to certain concessions to the South, among which was withdrawal of federal troops from that region. That meant that black rights could be violated with impunity. Reconstruction of the nation was over; the betrayal of black people had resumed.

1877-1896: From Alienation to Segregation

The Exodus of 1879. Many southern blacks responded to this turn of

All Colored People

THAT WANT TO

GO TO KANSAS,

On September 5th, 1877,

Can do so for $5.00

IMMIGRATION.

WHEREAS, We, the colored people of Lexington, Ky,. knowing that there is an abundance of choice lands now belonging to the Government, have assembled ourselves together for the purpose of locating on said lands. Therefore,

BE IT RESOLVED, That we do now organize ourselves into a Colony, as follows:— Any person wishing to become a member of this Colony can do so by paying the sum of one dollar ($1.00), and this money is to be paid by the first of September, 1877, in instalments of twenty-five cents at a time, or otherwise as may be desired.

RESOLVED. That this Colony has agreed to consolidate itself with the Nicodemus Towns, Solomon Valley, Graham County, Kansas, and can only do so by entering the vacant lands now in their midst, which costs $5.00.

RESOLVED, That this Colony shall consist of seven officers—President, Vice-President, Secretary, Treasurer, and three Trustees. President—M. M. Bell; Vice-President—Isaac Talbott; Secretary—W. J. Niles; Treasurer—Daniel Clarke; Trustees—Jerry Lee, William Jones, and Abner Webster.

RESOLVED, That this Colony shall have from one to two hundred militia, more or less, as the case may require, to keep peace and order, and any member failing to pay in his dues, as aforesaid, or failing to comply with the above rules in any particular, will not be recognized or protected by the Colony.

Land advertisement for forming a black colony in Kansas, 1877. (*Kansas Historical Society*)

events by fleeing the South for the "promised land" of Kansas. St. Louis, located on the Mississippi River, became a way station for the voyage to the West. By early March 1879, the first of the more than six thousand blacks who would come to St. Louis during the next four months arrived.

The problems faced by these exodusters, as the migrants were then known, were legion. The first obstacle to overcome was to secure money for boat fare up the Mississippi. It cost from three to four dollars per adult to travel from the vicinity of Vicksburg, Mississippi, to St. Louis. Children under ten years of age were transported for half price, and a small amount of baggage was carried free of charge. Consequently, a family of five needed from ten to fifteen dollars just to get up the river, an amount that, in many cases, blacks had to raise by a hasty and unprofitable sale of most of their household goods.

They arrived in St. Louis with their money spent and no way to secure passage to Kansas. The black community of St. Louis quickly responded to the exodusters' needs. The prominent black leader Charleton H. Tandy organized and spearheaded the relief effort. Tandy helped the men find jobs and arranged for impromptu food and shelter for the first group of several hundred who arrived in St. Louis on March 11, 1879. Tandy's efforts to solicit the aid of whites in St. Louis were largely unsuccessful. Indeed, St. Louis Mayor Henry Overstolz discouraged attempts to aid the migrants, lest other destitute southern blacks be attracted to his city. Realizing that whites were going to be of little help, Tandy organized a group of fifteen persons, later enlarged to a Committee of Twenty-five. The committee assumed the responsibility for seeing to the needs of the migrants, including the arrangement and supervision of their transportation to Kansas.

Most of the money raised in this relief venture came through the black churches of St. Louis. Between March 17 and April 22 alone, St. Louis blacks provided the exodusters with nearly three thousand dollars worth of goods and services, making it possible for the vast majority of them to move on to Kansas. Many migrants stopped again in Kansas City, where B. B. Watson, pastor of the African Methodist Episcopal Church, organized the relief effort. In contrast to his counterpart in St. Louis, Kansas City Mayor George M. Shelley supported the attempt to aid the freedmen.

Disappointment with the Republican Party. Blacks had supported the Radical Republican gubernatorial candidate, Joseph W. McClurg, in 1870. McClurg was defeated, however, after a split in the Republican party's ranks resulted in the formation of a coalition of Liberal Republicans and Democrats who joined to elect B. Gratz Brown Missouri's twentieth governor. He was replaced in 1872 by Silas Woodson of St. Joseph, a Democrat. During Woodson's two years in office, the Liberal Republican party quietly passed out of existence, assuring the Democrats control of the state legislature. A Republican Governor of Missouri was not elected again until Herbert S. Hadley took office in 1909.

Even if the Republicans had maintained control of state politics, blacks could have expected little from them. The endorsement of black political rights, which had been characteristic of the party in the late sixties, gave way to concern about economic issues in the seventies and eighties. In 1878 James Milton Turner, who had recently returned from a seven-year stint as Minister to Liberia, sought the Republican nomination for a congressional seat from Missouri's Third

District. Turner's candidacy was flatly rejected by the Republicans. So too was an effort to increase black representation on the Republican State Central Committee.

St. Louis was the only place in the state that blacks could expect any kind of support from the Republicans. There Chauncey I. Filley, longtime party leader and the St. Louis postmaster in the 1870s, appointed a few blacks to menial patronage positions in the post office. To many black Missourians, this feeble gesture was simply not enough.

The Missouri Republican Union. As the national election of 1880 approached, a delegation of black Missourians traveled to the White House for a meeting with President Rutherford B. Hayes. Led by James Milton Turner, these black leaders sought to persuade Hayes that the black vote in Missouri was still important and that the national Republicans should make greater efforts to reward their black supporters.

Lame-duck President Hayes did nothing, of course, and the black Missouri Republican Union turned its attention to his successor, James A. Garfield. Union members claimed that Garfield could not have been elected without the black vote. They then demanded patronage jobs for leaders of their race and protection for southern blacks. Turner and his colleagues tried to organize a national meeting in Washington, D. C., to dramatize their demands.

Despite efforts by Union members, the meeting in Washington never materialized, largely because many blacks in the country thought that such a gathering held little promise. Alternatively, the Missouri Republican Union turned its attention away from national politics and focused once again on affairs within the state. In August 1882, the Union sponsored a statewide black convention, held in Jefferson City.

One of the major objectives of this convention was for the state of Missouri to establish a mechanical or industrial school for black youths. A petition to that effect was presented to the House of Representatives, but it failed to gain the approval of the Committee on Education. The meeting in Jefferson City revealed a growing dissatisfaction among blacks with Republicanism. Members present passed what they called a "new Monroe Doctrine," announcing that the black vote could no longer be colonized and appropriated by the Republicans. Rather, blacks would henceforth support the party that showed the greatest promise of helping them.

Segregation. But there was no political party that showed any real interest in helping black people. Even the courts refused to offer any solace. In 1883 the United States Supreme Court declared the Civil

Rights Act of 1875 unconstitutional. The law of 1875, one of the last
vestiges of Radical Reconstruction, had attempted to ensure blacks
access to public accommodations such as restaurants and theaters.
Its nullification in 1883 touched off a series of new segregation legislation by the now-Democratically-controlled southern states that effectively deprived the freedmen of their constitutional rights.

Black Missourians had been fighting segregated education for
years. Missouri's constitution of 1875 left the issue of separate educational facilities vague. In 1881 black leaders James Milton Turner and
J. H. Murray met with Democratic Governor Thomas T. Crittenden in an
effort to encourage him to support integrated schools. Crittenden, however, refused to endorse any such move. Some schools continued to
admit both blacks and whites. In 1887, however, a white teacher in
Grundy County refused to admit black students to a white school which
had previously been open to them. Parents of the children sued the
teacher on the grounds that the young pupils were being denied rights
guaranteed to them by the Fourteenth Amendment.

While the courts debated the question, the Missouri legislature met
the issue head-on. In 1889 it passed a law ordering separate schools to
be established "for the children of African descent." The next year
the Grundy County case finally reached the Missouri Supreme Court.
The court ruled against the black students, and Justice Francis M. Black
wrote the unanimous decision. He declared that "color carries with it
natural race peculiarities" which justified the separation of blacks and
whites. Moreover, he proclaimed the court's opinion to be that these
race differences could never be eliminated. Six years later the United
States Supreme Court, in the famous Plessy v. Ferguson case, declared
separate but equal accommodations for blacks to be constitutional.
Segregation had become the law of the land, but the facilities were
unequal and separate. Although Missouri did not pass segregation
laws covering public accommodations, custom prohibited blacks from
joining whites in hotels, restaurants, theaters, hospitals, etc.

Urbanization and Black Political Loyalties

The Political Consequences of Urbanization. The black population of
Missouri changed dramatically during the last half of the nineteenth
century. Missouri's black population was moving to the cities. The
number of blacks in St. Louis increased six-fold between 1860 and
1870. By 1890, 47 percent of the state's black population lived in
cities; the figure jumped to 55 percent by 1900. Social, political and
economic changes for blacks came in the wake of these demographic
shifts.

The increased concentration of blacks in the cities, and the tendency of blacks in urban areas to congregate in a small area, comprising a few political wards, meant that if blacks voted together, they could influence city elections. Political leaders in Kansas City and St. Louis began to take notice of this change in 1890. In St. Louis, Dr. George Bryant, a black delegate to the St. Louis Republican convention, persuaded the delegates to nominate Walter M. Farmer, a black lawyer, for the position of Assistant Prosecuting Attorney for the Court of Criminal Correction. Another black man, W. C. Ball, was also nominated for the position of Constable. Both men were defeated by Democrats. Three years later, Farmer became the first black lawyer to argue a case on behalf of a black client before the Missouri Supreme Court.

In Kansas City there was a similar token acknowledgment of potential black political power. E. L. Hamlin, a wealthy black contractor, was nominated in 1890 for a seat on the city council. The Republican mayoral candidate, Joseph J. Davenport, endorsed Hamlin in return for the promise of black support at the polls. Both Hamlin and Davenport were defeated, however.

The nomination of three blacks for elective office in two Missouri cities certainly did not change the status of black people in the state. As the decade of the nineties wore on, the frustration and helplessness of blacks increased. The neglect of black people by political leaders led many lawless whites to feel that they had a license to harass them. This oppression was manifested most clearly in the growing prevalence of lynching in the state and nation during the late nineteenth and early twentieth centuries.

Lynching. The late nineteenth century was a violent period in American history. Industrialization spawned social and economic changes that shattered the agrarian life-style of the nation. Labor unrest, financial panics, and a tremendous increase in the number of immigrants who challenged native whites for jobs caused Americans to search for scapegoats for the country's problems. When scapegoats could be found, violence often occurred. Frequently it took the form of lynching, with blacks as the chief victims. Nationally, there were 3,224 persons lynched between 1889 and 1918, 2,522 of them black. During this same period there were eighty-one lynchings in Missouri. This was more than in the southern states of North Carolina (fifty-three) and Virginia (seventy-eight). It was much more than two states bordering Missouri: Illinois had twenty-four and Kansas twenty-two. Fifty-one of Missouri's lynching victims were black. Mob leaders generally escaped punishment, often with the connivance of legal authorities.

In 1892, a number of Missouri's most prominent black citizens

LYNCHINGS IN THE UNITED STATES, 1909-1918

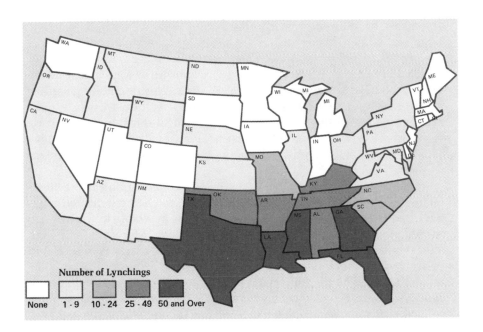

Number of Lynchings

None   1 - 9   10 - 24   25 - 49   50 and Over

called attention to the crime of violence. They hoped that educating whites to the realities of black life would make things better for them. James Milton Turner, Peter Clark, George B. Vashon, Walter Farmer, Albert Burgess, E. T. Cottman, Moses Dickson, R. H. Cole, P. H. Murray, John W. Wheeler, and a host of others circulated an address throughout the country, calling attention "to the wrongs that were being heaped upon" their fellow-blacks. They called for a national day of "humiliation, fasting, and prayer" to accent their plea. The date was set for May 31, 1892, and on that day St. Louis alone saw fifteen hundred blacks solemnly gather for what they called a "lamentation day."

Neither prayer nor fasting could stop lynching; indeed, such lawlessness increased. Perhaps the most flagrant example of this tragic violence against blacks occurred in Springfield in 1906. On Easter morning a mob of whites raided the local jail and removed three black prisoners. The three men were first shot, then burned, and finally hung from a statue of the goddess of liberty. The excitement surrounding this despicable event was so great that Governor Joseph Folk ordered the state militia into the city to quell the riot. The governor was eager to have the guilty parties sentenced to death and sent state officials to assist the local prosecuting attorney in the trial. After a lengthy trial, the leader of the mob was acquitted.

The Political Revolt of 1898. Despite the growing concentration of blacks in the cities, the Republican party continued to pay little attention to them. In 1892, former Radical William Warner ran for governor of Missouri on a "new Missouri" platform. The "new Missouri" program emphasized the state's need for industrial development and ignored black problems. In 1896, Chauncey Filley, bastion of patronage jobs for blacks in St. Louis, fell from power. Republican abandonment of blacks was complete.

As the elections of 1898 rolled around, black St. Louisans contemplated a break with their old political affiliates. They expected eight hundred of the eight thousand patronage jobs available in the city. Instead, they received only seventy-six in 1898. Moreover, although there were no black candidates in the city in 1898, blacks wanted David Murphy, a sympathetic judge of the Court of Criminal Corrections, renominated. The Republicans rejected their appeal. This defiance of blacks as a constituency prompted them to form an independent political organization and to move toward the Democratic party.

A slate of black candidates was offered for several elective positions and the Democrats, led by Governor Lon V. Stephens, began making overtures to the black rebels, but Democrats were themselves divided during these years. More and more Missouri farmers turned to third-party movements in the eighties and nineties. Obsessed with rolling back the power of encroaching industrialists, they advocated issues such as free silver and abandoned the party when it failed to take up their cry.

Internal squabbling caused perceptive Democrats to realize that the party needed new members. They quickly discovered that disaffected blacks could be wooed into the fold. Governor Stephens wrote to several black St. Louis leaders, hoping to sway them toward the Democrats. He promised patronage jobs to blacks, said he would do what he could to have blacks appointed as policemen, and advocated a strong antilynching law.

Stephens also concluded that he could gain black support by endorsing programs for Lincoln Institute in Jefferson City. He persuaded the legislature to appropriate money for a new dormitory. In return, he expected employees of the institute to form a nucleus of support for the Democratic party. The president of Lincoln Institute, Inman E. Page, refused to cooperate with Stephens, and he was quickly removed by the governor in 1898. Soon after the dismissal, support for Democratic candidates throughout the state came from the school.

Democrats dominated the election in black wards in Kansas City and St. Louis in 1898 and again in 1900. In St. Louis, Democratic ward boss Ed Butler and his son Jim organized black support. They were aided by a new machine organization in the city run by St. Louis Police Board Commissioner Harry B. Hawes and known as the Jefferson Club. Through Hawes's efforts, an auxiliary Negro Jefferson Club was formed, with C. C. Rankin, Crittenden Clark, W. II. Fields, and James Milton Turner as leaders.

The Negro Jefferson Club rallied behind Democrat Rolla Wells and helped him win the mayoral contest in St. Louis in 1901. In Kansas City, blacks organized a Negro Central League and supported James Reed, a Pendergast organization's candidate for mayor. Reed won the contest and gave a number of jobs in the fire department to blacks.

White Reaction and Political Uncertainty. The growing influence of blacks on urban Democrats was more than the rural members of the party could take. Racism among this so-called Confederate faction had always been present, but it soared to new heights in the early twentieth century. In 1903, rural Democrats tried to pass new segregation laws, particularly for railroad travel. Urban Democrats joined with Republicans to defeat the bill.

Despite their loss on the issue of segregation, rural Democrats remained strong in the party and made race a political issue in 1904. Democratic antiblack rhetoric, combined with Theodore Roosevelt's open courting of the black vote and the unfulfilled promises of the Democrats, caused many blacks to return to the Republican fold. Consequently, Democratic urban machine organizations declined in power during these years. The rural Democrats attempted to capitalize on the decline and tried repeatedly but unsuccessfully to pass segregation laws and to limit the ability of blacks to vote. This process was not reversed again until the revival of the big city bosses in 1910.

The election of Republican Governor Herbert S. Hadley in 1908 brought a more favorable state response to the plight of blacks than had existed for nearly forty years. Hadley appointed blacks to patronage jobs, made efforts to improve the health of black Missourians, and fought strongly against lynching. But blacks were not to be so easily bought off this time. They realized that white restrictions on where they lived gave them a power base in the cities. In St. Louis, black leaders Joseph E. Mitchell, Charles Turpin, Homer G. Phillips, and George L. Vaughn formed the Citizens Liberty League to endorse black candidates. Turpin was elected a constable.

Political bosses and party machines dominated city affairs from 1910 to 1920: the Republicans in St. Louis and the Democrats in Kansas City. The increasingly urbanized blacks of the state found themselves more and more closely attached to these machines. Still, the masses of blacks received few benefits from either party.

The Social Consequences of Urbanization

Slums and Health. The movement of blacks into narrowly-defined sections of cities meant more than that their votes could be the deciding factor in closely contested elections: it meant that they were thrust together in terribly overcrowded neighborhoods. By 1910 nearly 67 percent of Missouri's blacks lived in cities, almost three times the national average. They were confined to crowded urban ghettos, where unsanitary conditions, crime, and vice prevailed. In the 1890s blacks in St. Louis lived in areas where the population density averaged eighty-two people per acre, as opposed to the overall city average of only twelve people per acre.

Slum districts took on characters of their own, and became known by such descriptive names as "Clabber Alley," "Wild Cat Chute," and "Hog Alley." In 1882, Jefferson City's Hog Alley was quarantined when a local physician mistakenly diagnosed smallpox among alley residents. Local officials placed armed guards at entrances to the alley, hopeful of preventing spread of the disease throughout the city. Subsequently, the physician's erroneous diagnosis was revealed, although the scare created a public outcry for something to be done about the filth and squalor of Hog Alley. A local newspaper offered this assessment.

> Hog alley to Jefferson City is what Clabber alley is to St. Louis. It is a disgrace to the city; all that is filthy, low, mean and vicious of the colored population can at one time and another be found in this alley. It reeks with filth and crime and wickedness. In its confines are to be found the vagabonds, thieves and prostitutes of the colored population. Innumerable cutting and shooting scrapes, broils and rows of all kinds and varieties have occurred there. The recent scare about the smallpox had its origin there and attracted the attention of the whole city to it. Now is a good time to talk about what action should be taken to rid the city of this blot. The old rookeries of the alley should be declared nuisances by the city authorities and abated if it can be done; if not, the city should buy the old houses and tear them down. We don't know who they belong to, but whoever owns them owes it as a duty to their fellow-citizens not to rent them to the vile class that now occupy them and bring disgrace upon the city.

Soon after, the city council did authorize the razing of several alley buildings. In Kansas City, as late as 1915, most blacks lived in the tenement houses located on "The Bowery." Most of the buildings there were two- and three-story brick structures, arranged in two- and three-room apartments. Nearly all were poorly constructed and crowded closely together, many of them facing the alleys. One indication of over-crowding is evidenced by the fact that twenty-two blocks in that area had a population of 4,295. In Southeast Missouri and in semi-rural places and small towns, housing was even worse.

Substandard housing greatly increased the need for health services for blacks, while low incomes made it difficult for them to purchase these services. White physicians often refused to take care of black patients and hospitals refused to admit them. Consequently, black doctors set up their own hospitals, usually in former private dwellings. In November 1910, Dr. J. E. Perry set up such a hospital in Kansas City, called the Perry Sanitarium and Nurse Training Association. In 1915 it became Provident Hospital and Nurse Training Association. Its name was changed to Wheatly-Provident Hospital in 1916.

But these hospitals were unable to deal with the health problems of urbanized blacks. Proportionately, many more blacks were dying and at younger ages than were whites. In 1911, for example, Kansas City officials commissioned a report on the health of the city's citizens, a study which covered a period of seven months. During each of those seven months, deaths exceeded births among blacks. The black population of the city was actually declining, while the white growth rate was 15 percent.

Part of the reason for the decline was that many blacks fled from the terrible living conditions in which they found themselves by leaving the state. During the thirty years from 1880 to 1910, Missouri's black population showed a net increase of only 12,102. The black population of the state actually decreased by 3,782 (2.3 percent) during the decade of 1900 to 1910. The white population grew by 6.5 percent during the same period.

Black Achievements

Black Organizations. Those who stayed tried to cope in a variety of ways. State chapters of newly formed national organizations such as the Urban League and the National Association for the Advancement of Colored People (NAACP) came to the urban areas. They advocated improved job opportunities and better legal and social services for blacks. Many blacks turned inward, to members of their own race, to solve their problems. Black fraternal groups and lodges became extremely popular during these years. They provided blacks with social cohesion and solidarity. These groups tried to take care of their destitute members, providing relief when it was unavailable elsewhere. Americans, during these years, generally took the position that public funds should not be used to support unemployed, elderly, and infirm people who could not take care of themselves. The Ancient Free and Accepted Masons of Missouri therefore established a Masonic Home near Hannibal, Missouri, in 1908. The home cared for elderly and impoverished Masons and orphans of Masons. It remained a mainstay of the Masonic community until the mid-twentieth century.

Black Businesses. The same sentiment toward racial solidarity that caused the lodges to flourish also contributed to the prosperity of a number of black businesses which catered almost exclusively to a segregated clientele. There were many black businessmen and professionals in St. Louis especially. Charles C. Clark ran Clark and Smith Men's Furnishing Goods Store, H. S. Ferguson owned the successful St. Louis Delicatessen Company, and C. K. Robinson was proprietor of the Robinson Printing Company. Yearly sales of black businesses such as these totaled more than one million dollars. Yet this impressive figure represented only about 8 percent of the estimated annual earnings of black St. Louisans. More than 90 percent of the black wage earners worked as personal servants, factory workers, and common laborers.

In outstate Missouri, most rural blacks were still engaged in farming. State statistics revealed that Missouri blacks owned nearly thirty-eight hundred farms in 1913 for an estimated worth of $27,768,750. In that same year, B. K. Bruce, a black farmer and educator who was the head of the Bartlett Agricultural and Industrial School for Negroes in Chariton County, won the premium for the United States on corn shown at the San Francisco Exposition.

Black Newspapers. Black newspapers of this era catered to and tried to increase black togetherness in the face of oppression. Publishers of black newspapers usually had very limited capital with which to start. Consequently, they were often shortlived enterprises. One of the most successful of the black newspapers during these years was the St. Louis *Palladium,* founded in 1884 and edited by John W. Wheeler from 1897 to 1911. Wheeler advocated black advancement through industry and self-help, a philosophy eminently consistent with that of his contemporary, Booker T. Washington, a national black leader. Wheeler shied away from the politics of confrontation and refused to abandon the Republican party when others of his race were doing so in the nineties and the early years of the twentieth century.

John "Blind" Boone and his wife.
(State Historical Society of Missouri)

Black Music. Perhaps one of the most positive contributions of the
years of betrayal was the flowering of black music in the segregated
honky-tonks and dance halls of the state. John William "Blind" Boone
of Warrensburg was a musical phenomenon. Born in 1864, he was attacked with what was described as "brain fever" when only six months
old. A Warrensburg doctor removed his eyes to relieve the pressure on
his brain. Boone began playing publicly while still in his teens, and in
1879 he was taken to Columbia by John Lange, Jr., a black contractor
who managed him for thirty-five years. Boone had the uncanny ability
to reproduce, note for note, even the most complicated pieces after only

"Blind" Boone concert company.
(State Historical Society of Missouri)

Scott Joplin. *(Kansas City Times)*

one hearing. Current musicologists believe that Boone's music, some of which is preserved today on player-piano rolls, reveals much about early ragtime music.

Blind Boone's better known contemporary, Scott Joplin, lived for several years in Sedalia and later moved to St. Louis. Joplin was born in 1868 and left home to become a pianist at age fourteen. Two of his most famous pieces were "The Maple Leaf Rag" and "Treemonisha." The latter is an opera in which education is offered as the key to social advancement of black people. Other of these turn-of-the century black musicians from St. Louis included Tom Turpin and W. C. Handy. It was Handy who composed the still-popular "St. Louis Blues."

The Frustrations of Segregation

Perhaps Handy's title sums up the feeling of Missouri blacks generally during these years. It was a mournful period. By the time America entered the First World War, blacks were leaving the state in inordinately large numbers. Those who remained became increasingly urbanized, moving to the cities to find jobs and upward social mobility. Instead, most found segregation and squalor and, at best, an uneasy alliance with machine politicians.

St. Louis tried desperately to segregate blacks in 1916. Local citizens, unable to work effectively through the party machinery, used the initiative-referendum procedure to place a segregation ordinance on the ballot. St. Louisans passed the ordinance by a three to one majority, although it was later declared unconstitutional by the United States Supreme Court.

Despite the court's ruling, the sentiment of white St. Louis and the rest of Missouri toward blacks was obvious. A report in 1914 by the Missouri Association for Social Welfare summed up the situation. Writing for the association, white Missourian Roger Baldwin declared that "so much of the problem lies in the unthinking, inconsiderate attitude of white people that no specific remedies for present conditions can be proposed which in themselves offer any solution." The future looked bleak indeed.

SUGGESTED READINGS

The exodus of 1879 has been the subject of numerous books and articles, among them the following: Nell Irving Painter, *Exodusters: Black Migration to Kansas After Reconstruction* (New York, 1977),

Susanna M. Grenz, "The Exodusters of 1879: St. Louis and Kansas City Responses," *Missouri Historical Review,* LXXIII (October 1978), pages 54-79, andArvarh E. Strickland, "Toward the Promised Land: The Exodus to Kansas and Afterward," *Missouri Historical Review,* LXIX (July 1975), pages 376-412.

Black education during this period is covered in W. Sherman Savage, "The Legal Provisions for Negro Schools in Missouri from 1865 to 1890," *Journal of Negro History,* XXVI (July 1931), pages 309-321. Information about the black press can be gleaned from the following articles: George Everett Slavens, "The Missouri Negro Press 1875-1920," *Missouri Historical Review,* LXIV (July 1970), pages 413-431, and Lawrence O. Christensen, "The Racial Views of John W. Wheeler," *Missouri Historical Review,* LXVII (July 1973), pages 535-547.

The story behind Missouri blacks' involvement in the development of ragtime music is told in Rudi Blesh and Harriet Jonis, *They All Played Ragtime, the True Story of an American Music* (New York, 1950).

8

Hope Betrayed:

Between the World Wars

The era of World War I brought alternate hope and disillusionment for black Americans. The war effort required all Americans, blacks included, to make sacrifices in winning the struggle. When the war ended, blacks expected to share equally in the fruits of victory. Instead, they found that their state and nation grew increasingly hostile toward them in the twenties. Likewise, when economic depression struck in the thirties, they found that they were hit the hardest.

World War I

Black Soldiers in the War. World War I was to have been a particularly idealistic confrontation. President Woodrow Wilson proclaimed its noble purpose when he declared that it was "a war to end all wars." Hoping for full citizenship, black Americans, Missourians included, took part in the struggle, but only after being urged by black leaders, especially W. E. B. DuBois. Many blacks believed that prejudice against them would be lessened if they joined the fight. Less than twenty years before, that sentiment had led a number of black Missourians to volunteer for service in the Spanish American War. The

First payday in Cuba for 9th and 10th Cavalry. *(State Historical Society of Missouri)*

black "70th Regiment of the Immunes" was mustered in on September 16, 1898, at St. Louis with 42 officers and 953 enlisted men.

The first World War saw a similar response from the black community. Nationwide, 404,348 blacks joined the army. This total included 1,353 commissioned officers, 9 field clerks, and 15 army nurses. There were 9,219 black Missouri soldiers inducted into the service between June 5, 1917 and November 11, 1918. Despite his willingness to fight, however, the black soldier was used primarily as a noncombatant, usually in transportation, loading and unloading ships, driving trucks, etc. When he did receive an opportunity to fight, he acquitted himself well. Two black infantry divisions, the 92d and 93d, served in France. The 92d Division served on the battlefront with the U.S. Second Army in an assault on the Hindenburg line. In September 1918, the *Crisis* carried the following assessment of black soldiers in a recent battle:

> American Negro troops proved their value as fighters in the line east of Verdun on June 12. . . . The Germans attempted a raid in that sector but were completely repulsed by the Negroes. The Boches began a terrific bombardment at one minute after midnight (throwing over between 3,000 and 4,000 shells from guns ranging in size from 67 to 340 millimeters). The bombardment was concentrated on small areas. Many of the shells made holes from ten to fifteen feet across. In the midst of this inferno

the Negroes cooly stuck to their posts, operating machine guns and automatic rifles and keeping up such a steady barrage that the German infantry failed to penetrate the American lines. The Americans miraculously sustained only two wounded.

Obviously, the black soldier was fighting for a victory that was both national and personal; he wanted victory for America and hoped that upon his return he would receive the full rights of citizenship that had thus far eluded him.

Tapping Black Resources at Home. When the war broke out, Democratic Governor Frederick D. Gardner asked a number of black leaders in the state about how blacks could become a more efficient and productive part of the state and nation. Tired of the lack of response to their problems from both Democrats and Republicans, a number of leaders responded that black self-help was the only answer. They proposed the idea of a Missouri Negro Industrial Commission, run by blacks, that would allow black citizens to prove their merit. The Commission would try to unite blacks around a program of character building, hard work, and thrift in an effort to prove to the white majority their readiness for full rights of citizenship. Gardner responded in February 1918 by creating the Missouri State Negro Industrial Commission.

The commission immediately latched on to the war as a vehicle for proving the black commitment to America. It encouraged black Missouri farmers to increase their agricultural production. Likewise, it pleaded with blacks all over the state to work hard, and not to waste time or food. It speculated that these encouragements would save the state more than $150,000. Likewise, the commission persuaded Missouri blacks to buy $600,000 worth of Liberty Bonds, despite their general poverty.

The Migration of Black Population

New Urban Opportunities for Blacks. The war gave blacks all over the country an opportunity to improve their conditions. When fighting broke out in 1914, European immigration, averaging approximately one million people a year, virtually stopped. With Europe torn apart by the war, the United States became the workshop of the world. White employers, badly in need of workers for mines, railroads, shipyards, automobile factories, flour and meat packing houses, turned to a major new source of labor—the southern blacks.

Blacks began to stream North by the thousands to fill the labor gap. Census figures revealed that in 1910 there were 552,845 blacks in

NEGRO POPULATION OF KANSAS CITY/ST. LOUIS, 1890-1940

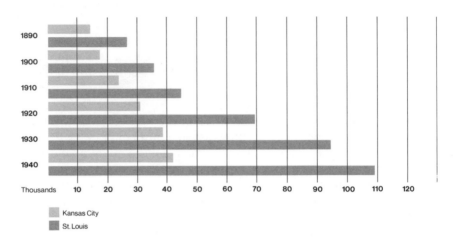

the country engaged in industrial pursuits; that number jumped to 960,039 by 1920. Many idle or underpaid Missouri blacks left the state for Detroit, Pittsburgh, New York, Cleveland, and Chicago, where they could earn five dollars a day in factories, foundries, and shipyards. Rural blacks hearing of better economic and social opportunities in the cities moved to Kansas City and St. Louis, where they went to work for factories, railroads, and in other jobs.

The Black Population Spills into White Areas. What was to happen at the war's end to all of the black migrants who had been attracted by urban industry? They stayed in the cities, adding to the general unemployment which the end of hostilities had raised to dangerously high levels. Greater numbers of blacks living in cities meant that two things would happen. First, the all-black neighborhoods of the cities became more crowded, more unsanitary, and more crime-ridden. Second, the all-black neighborhoods could no longer contain all of the blacks seeking housing, so that more and more they began seeking places to live in formerly all-white neighborhoods. Many white families resented living next door to blacks. Some moved away; others threatened black families. Still others resorted to violence. A period of extreme reaction set in: "outsiders"—immigrants, Jews, Communists, blacks, and a host of others outside the mainstream of American life—were attacked as alien to the American way.

Violent Reactions. Such black movements into white neighborhoods

NAACP advertisement. *(State Historical Society of Missouri)*

were often vigorously resisted. In 1905 pastors of five white churches in St. Louis joined together to stop the sale of the white Central Presbyterian Church to the black congregation of Memorial Methodist Episcopal Church. In 1908 a white St. Louis newspaper carried the following headline: "The Negro Must Go, Is Cry: West End Citizens Bitterly Resent Invasion of Blacks." In 1925, Samuel R. Hopkins, the black president of the Square Deal Realty and Loan Company, tried to move into a formerly all-white neighborhood in Kansas City. His home was bombed.

One of the bloodiest confrontations in the country occurred in East St. Louis, just across the river from Missouri's largest city. Ten thousand black migrants had come to the city, many searching for jobs in factories holding government contracts. In at least one instance, rural blacks were actually imported into the city by white businessmen to break a strike. Clashes between white and black workers ended in a bloody race riot in July 1917. Before it was over, forty to two hundred blacks had been killed. Across the river, tensions also ran high, but St. Louis managed to avoid a similar racial explosion.

Lynching continued to be the favorite weapon of hostile and lawless whites. One of the most brutal lynchings ever in the state occurred at Charleston in 1924. In that year, a black man named Roosevelt Grigsley was lynched by a mob of two hundred men who took him from law enforcement officials. He was hanged in front of a grocery store; shots were fired through his body and later he was tied behind a car and dragged through the streets of the black section of town. A

1923 lynching in Columbia, Missouri, led to the establishment of a chapter of the National Association for the Advancement of Colored People (NAACP) in Jefferson City.

The Twenties

Self-Help, Self-Expression. Opposition to black laborers led many workers to try to form labor unions and bargain collectively. Unions such as the Negro Brotherhood of Sleeping Car Porters and Maids, under the Socialist labor leader A. Phillip Randolph, tried to organize black workers. In 1914, there were 900 black Pullman porters in St. Louis, the largest block of black railroad workers in the city. But the Pullman Company threatened to fire workers who joined the union, a threat that was carried out on more than one occasion in St. Louis and Kansas City. Black workers still had too little influence to make black labor unions a powerful force. As late as 1929, there were still only eighty-one St. Louis blacks in Randolph's union.

The twenties also saw a renewed interest in black culture and black consciousness. This was, in large part, a response to the continuing overt discrimination. A number of black writers such as W. E. B. DuBois, James Weldon Johnson, Claude McKay, Jean Toomer, Countee Cullen, Langston Hughes, and a host of others, wrote of both racial pride and oppression. Hughes, a native of Joplin, Missouri, became one of the most prolific and famous. His books *Weary Blues* and *Fine Clothes to the Jews* in the twenties assured him lasting literary recognition.

This movement, centered in New York City and known as the "Harlem Renaissance," extended to Missouri, primarily in the form of a musical revolution. Ragtime music gave way to the Jazz Age, and Missouri blacks helped to point the way. Perhaps Missouri's most famous jazz musician of the "Jumping Twenties" was Will "Count" Basie who came to Kansas City as a penniless piano player in mid-decade. Basie joined the Bennie Moten band and sent jazz music to new heights. The Count described his own style of music as follows: "I don't dig the two-beat jive the New Orleans cats play, because my boys and I got to have four heavy beats to a bar and no cheating." When Moten died in 1928, Count Basie took the band and carried it to international acclaim.

The Hope Offered by Education. Most Missouri blacks still hoped that education would be the key to winning first-class citizenship. But nowhere was discrimination more firmly entrenched than in education. In 1917 the state had approximately 926,000 blacks and was spending

Bennie Moten Orchestra, Kansas City, 1931. Count Basie is third from right.
(Kansas City Star)

$1,764,334 per year on black education. By contrast, the District of Columbia had only 64,868 blacks but was spending $1,660,206 on their education or a little over thirteen times as much per person. In Sedalia, black teachers were paid $785 per year in 1919-1920, while white teachers in comparable schools were paid $1,108.

Inadequate facilities were also the rule. Some schools used by Missouri blacks in the twenties were so bad that black paint was applied to wooden walls to substitute for blackboards. Schools were often overcrowded, some seating as many as three students to a desk. Others could afford no desks and seated students on benches of rough hewn wood. One school had no water supply within 200 yards.

State Superintendent Charles A. Lee resolved to improve the educational opportunities of blacks when he assumed his position in 1923. Legislation in 1921 had begun to point the way. An Inspector of Negro Schools was authorized and provisions were made for the establishment of black high schools in Missouri counties having a population of one hundred thousand or more. White support for these measures was somewhat self-interested, however. Lee's predecessor pleaded with county superintendents to support black education because, in his words, "illiteracy . . . breeds contempt for law and order and lays the foundations for anarchy and bolshevism."

About all that the Inspector of Negro Schools could do, however, was to document the terrible inadequacy of Missouri's black schools. The single most important problem was the expense of trying to maintain a separate but equal educational system, one for blacks and one for whites. Missouri simply could not afford it. Inspector N. C. Bruce summed up the situation in his 1924 report.

> Six Missouri counties have no Negro persons at all, sixteen other counties have less than ten, forty counties have only seven-hundred Negro population, with 243 children in groups from 1 to 8, 12 and 14, not enough for the legal 15 for starting a colored school. Neither, in many counties, do the boards of education feel financially able to run two public schools. Missouri's poor school districts cannot maintain separate race schools except at great disparity and inequality.

The only solution was a single integrated system.

Blacks and Politics in the Twenties. The increasing urbanization of Missouri's blacks tied them more closely than ever before to the urban political machines. In St. Louis, the Republican party dominated and blacks tended to stay with that party, although there was continuous dissatisfaction with the lack of responsiveness from the old party of Lincoln. Democrats, under the leadership of Tom Pendergast, controlled Kansas City and blacks there generally sided with them. Statewide, blacks still tended to support the Republican party, although, again, that was changing. The Republicans failed to resolve problems for blacks during the years they controlled the governor's office from 1921 to 1933, thus adding to the number of alienated and frustrated blacks.

Blacks in St. Louis were becoming better organized by 1920. The nucleus of their group was an organization known as the Citizens Liberty League. The league, aided by the Statewide Missouri Negro Republican League, was able to gain the nomination and election of Walthall Moore in 1920. Moore was the first black man to serve in the Missouri Legislature. He lost his bid for reelection in 1922, but St. Louis blacks did see Crittenden Clark become the first black justice of the peace in the city while Charles Turpin and Langston Harrison were elected constables.

Of major concern to blacks in the twenties was the rising influence of the Ku Klux Klan. The Klan enjoyed a general revival in America in that decade, tapping the reservoir of resentment against change that was building in the country and attacking everything that was not "one hundred percent American." The Klan reached the height of its influence in the state in the 1924 election. Arthur Davis, Democratic gubernatorial candidate, refused to sign an affidavit denying member-

Ten Reasons Why You Should Be A Member of N. A. A. C. P.

The Association is fighting against:

1. Lynching of Negroes.
2. Disfranchisement of colored Voters in South.
3. The Ku Klux Klan.
4. Peonage, Industrial Slavery.
5. Jim Crow Cars.
6. The Chain Gang.
7. Dynamiting Negroes Homes.

The Association is fighting for:

8. Defense of the Arkansas riots Victims.
9. Opening trades to Negroes.
10. Better schools for Negro Children.

Join today and help the cause.

NAACP advertisement. (*State Historical Society of Missouri*)

ship in the Klan and admitted that he had attended a Klan rally near his home. Republican candidate Sam Baker, on the other hand, willingly signed such a statement and spoke out against the Klan. Baker was elected and received the majority of Missouri's black votes. St. Louis voters also returned Walthall Moore to the General Assembly in 1924 and chose Robert T. Scott as the first black ward committeeman.

Despite this apparent merger of black and Republican interests, however, all was not well between the traditional allies. Blacks expected more control of their own affairs; instead, they were getting less.

Lincoln Institute, Jefferson City, Missouri. *(State Historical Society of Missouri)*

They became particularly upset when Governor Baker tried to interfere with the administration of Lincoln Institute, only recently made into a university as a result of legislation sponsored by Representative Moore. After repeated efforts, Baker succeeded in ousting the popular president of Lincoln University, Nathan B. Young. That action, combined with Baker's failure to curtail lynchings and the party's unwillingness to support a black congressional candidate, further frustrated blacks.

As the election of 1928 approached, the Kansas City Pendergast organization used its influence on the Democratic party to tap this frustration. Among other things, the Democrats nominated black St. Louisan Joseph L. McLemore for Congress. Despite McLemore's loss, his nomination and support by Democrats impressed blacks and pointed the way toward the thirties when the black Missouri vote would become solidly Democratic.

The Thirties

Blacks and the Depression. The stock market crash of 1929 sent the American economy in a downward plunge from which it would not

Tenement homes, St. Louis, 1937. (*Charles Trefts Collection, State Historical Society of Missouri*)

recover for more than a decade. Millions of Americans, used to relative comfort and security, had to face unemployment, handouts, and even soup lines. The Great Depression hit blacks hardest of all. They were the last to be hired and the first to be fired. Whites now openly competed for jobs that were once regarded as "nigger" tasks. The trend was reflected even in the state capitol, where white elevator operators replaced blacks.

White labor unions, traditionally hostile to black workers, became even more so in the thirties. Black organizations attempted to create jobs. The Kansas City Urban League, for example, opened a training school for janitors and graduated its first class in 1934. The hardest hit were the sharecroppers of the Bootheel, in Southeast Missouri. Both white and black tenants of this region were forced to live in crude shacks that were unpainted and lacked plastering and insulation. In 1936 white sharecroppers in the Bootheel could expect to make a little over $400 for the year, while blacks had to settle for approximately $150 less.

In 1939 nearly 300 men, women, and children were facing death by exposure and starvation in a shack colony near Poplar Bluff. They were denied federal relief by local officials who were controlled by the white planters of the area. Many in the colony were the remnants of fifteen hundred black and white cotton pickers who had earlier resisted eviction by the planters. The cotton pickers had been led by Owen R. Whitfield, black preacher and labor organizer.

The New Deal and Missouri Blacks. President Franklin D. Roosevelt's New Deal social welfare programs offered some respite from the economic woes. To begin with, Roosevelt's appointment of several blacks to responsible positions created a degree of optimism. In 1934 he named Dr. William J. Thompkins, well-known Kansas City physician and politician, as recorder of deeds for the District of Columbia. This was Thompkins' reward for helping to swing black votes to the Roosevelt camp in the election of 1932. The president also appointed newspaperman Lester A.Walton, a native of St. Louis, to the position of minister to Liberia. At the time of his appointment in 1935, Walton was associate editor of the *New York Age.*

Further encouragement was given blacks by the formation of a "Black Cabinet" in the Roosevelt administration, consisting of brilliant individuals such as William Hastie, Robert Weaver, Ralph Bunche, B. T. McGraw, and Mary Bethune. Public works projects using federal funds to perform socially beneficial tasks, such as the building of hospitals, schools, and playgrounds, offered employment to blacks. In 1938, a $3,160,000 black hospital, built with the aid of a New Deal program, was dedicated in St. Louis and named for black attorney Homer G. Phillips, who had worked to ensure its existence before his assassination. Ironically, white unions kept black laborers from working on this job. One program especially useful to blacks, both nationally and locally, was the Civilian Conservation Corps. This program took thousands of young people off the streets and set them to work reforesting denuded lands. The National Youth Administration, under the leadership of Mrs. Bethune, enabled students and others, particularly at Lincoln University, to secure a college education or learn trades. The Social Security Act of 1935 provided for old age pensions and unemployment insurance, both of which were a boon to blacks.

Racial Tension in the Thirties. But if relief measures were offering some hope to blacks, competition for the nation's limited economic resources added to already-existing tensions between blacks and whites. In 1930, state troopers were twice called into the little town of Ste. Genevieve to put down racial violence. The entire black population, with the exception of two families, left town after the whites made threats. In 1933 a mob in St. Joseph murdered and then burned a nineteen-year-old black prisoner after the sheriff gave him up. Reportedly, women and children cheered as the victim's eyes were gouged out.

A reign of terror swept Missouri during the election of 1934. In March, the municipal election was marred by the slaying of a black Democratic precinct captain. Eleven others were injured in the bloodiest and most fiercely contested balloting in the city's history. Within a week, gunmen trying to prevent blacks from voting terrorized the southwest community of Holland, climaxing a series of antiblack demonstrations which had recently occurred elsewhere in that part of the state.

In 1939, racial friction broke out between blacks and whites in the small town of Oran. The trouble developed around a dispute over the right-of-way on a sidewalk. A mob decided to run all blacks out of town. State troopers were called in when the mob nearly destroyed a black family's house.

Persistent Segregation in Missouri. Segregation was still the rule in Missouri in the thirties. On the positive side, this allowed a number of black entrepreneurs, particularly those in service industries catering primarily to the black population, to enjoy financial success. Mrs. Annie Malone established a beauty culture business in St. Louis and amassed a fortune of more than a million dollars. She was the founder and owner of the Poro Beauty College in St. Louis and the chief benefactor of a black orphanage that still bears her name. A number of black insurance companies also thrived. The Douglass Life Insurance Company, started in 1919, with home offices in St. Louis, by 1923 had over twenty thousand policy owners in Missouri. It did business in twenty cities and towns in Missouri, in addition to St. Louis and Kansas City. The company had developed an annual premium income of $38,000 in four years, and had the distinction of being the first insurance company in the state financed and managed exclusively by blacks. Jefferson City got its first black law firm in 1933 when Robert J. Cobb, W. Franklin Clark, and Sidney Redmond opened an office.

But the disadvantages of segregation far outweighed any financial advantages gained by a few black businesses. Everywhere in the state blacks were treated as second-class citizens. In 1930, J. G. Ish, Jr., a black man, was refused a seat on the Pickwick-Greyhound night coach between Kansas City and St. Louis. Prospective black jurors were systematically kept out of jury service in the thirties. St. Louis had twenty-one higher educational facilities in 1934, and only two of them—one a normal school and the other a nurses' training school—would admit blacks. Of the city's eighty-four recreational centers, only ten were open to blacks, and four of those were segregated. Seven out of seventy swimming pools and playgrounds were open to black St. Louisans. Segregation even invaded the world of

Annie Turnbo Malone. *(Chicago Historical Society)*

sports. In April 1939, the University of Missouri was forced to cancel plans for a triangular track meet with the University of Wisconsin and Notre Dame. Wisconsin withdrew when Missouri banned its black hurdler, Ed Smith. Notre Dame then pulled out of the meet in protest.

Inroads against segregation occurred, however. In January 1938, black professor E. O. Borne won a five hundred dollar lawsuit against the segregation policies of the Pickwick-Greyhound Bus Line. And in that same month, white and black citizens worshiped jointly at an inter-racial religious program in Moberly.

Education: The First Major Challenge to Segregation

The most exciting challenges to segregation, however, came in the field of education. It was becoming increasingly obvious that the state could not provide "separate but equal" educational facilities for less than 10 percent of the state's population. The issue came to a head dramatically in demands for black graduate education in Missouri in the thirties. The famous Lloyd Gaines case started with a Lincoln University student and ended with a United States Supreme Court decision that struck at the foundation of the state and nation's segregated schools.

Lloyd Gaines graduated from Lincoln University in 1936. He applied for admission to the University of Missouri Law School, but was turned down because he was black. Gaines, with the aid of NAACP attorneys, sued the school, but Missouri's courts upheld the university's position. Gaines then appealed his case to the United States Supreme Court. That body, which had been made more liberal by the advent of Roosevelt appointees, ruled in favor of Gaines by a six to two vote.

Chief Justice Hughes, writing for the majority, declared that the State of Missouri had either to admit Lloyd Gaines to the all-white Missouri Law School, or provide truly equal facilities for Gaines and other blacks to pursue legal careers. The end of the era of shuttling blacks off to separate and inferior educational facilities had begun. Ironically, Gaines disappeared before the Supreme Court handed down its mandate; he has not been heard from since.

Although the Gaines case would point the way for future developments in black-white relations, the state of Missouri was not yet ready to give up its segregationist policies. Consequently, rather than allow blacks to enroll at the University of Missouri, it decided to set up a law school for blacks through Lincoln University. Thus, Lincoln University Law School—poorly-funded, understaffed, and ill-equipped— came into existence in St. Louis during the summer of 1940.

The Gaines challenge to segregated education in Missouri was followed by a similar effort on the part of Lucille Bluford in 1939. Ms. Bluford, the managing editor of the *Kansas City Call*, sought admission to the University of Missouri's world-famous School of Journalism. Again, the university and the state declined to admit a black person to its campus. Instead, it created in 1941 the Lincoln University School of Journalism. The degree to which the state was willing to go to avoid integrating the University of Missouri can be seen in the legislature's first-year appropriation for the Lincoln University School of Journalism: $65,000 for three students!

The Gaines and Bluford cases did not, of course, cause an immediate groundswell for integration in the state. They did, however, lay the groundwork for the overturn of the 1890s doctrine of the "separate but equal" discriminatory doctrine of *Plessy v. Ferguson*. Henceforth, Missouri's response to its black community would be increasingly open to challenge. Black-white relations could never again be the same.

SUGGESTED READINGS

The best work on this period is a doctoral dissertation completed at the University of Missouri in 1970 by Larry H. Grothaus: "The Negro in Missouri Politics, 1890-1914." This study may be ordered directly from University Microfilms, Ann Arbor, Michigan.

The urban migration of blacks during the war years is covered in Emmet J. Scott, *Negro Migration During the War* (New York, 1920). The economic status of black St. Louis is the subject of William A. Crossland, *Industrial Conditions Among Negroes in St. Louis* (St. Louis, 1914).

The role of the Ku Klux Klan in Missouri is dealt with briefly in Kenneth Jackson, *The Ku Klux Klan in the City 1915-1930* (New York, 1976). Larry Grothaus reveals much about the movement of Missouri blacks to the Democratic machine, in "Kansas City Blacks, Harry S Truman and the Pendergast Machine," *Missouri Historical Review,* LXVIII (October 1974), pages 65-82.

General information about blacks and the New Deal, with some references to Missouri, is available in Raymond Wolters, *Negroes and the Great Depression* (Westport, Conn., 1970). Louis Cantor, "A Prologue to the Protest Movement: The Missouri Sharecroppers Roadside Demonstration of 1939," *Journal of American History,* LV (March 1969), pages 804-822, is also helpful.

The rise of the Jazz Age in Missouri is dealt with in William H. Young and Nathan B. Young, *Your Kansas City and Mine* (Kansas City, 1950).

Appeal for Justice:
Segregation Challenged

As the decade of the forties began, American citizens anxiously watched from afar Adolf Hitler's challenge to Europe. In December 1941, of course, the United States became involved in what had ballooned into World War II. Ultimately, the war had a dramatic effect on black life in America. It opened new job possibilities and provided blacks with an opportunity to demonstrate again the importance of their role in American society. But despite their involvement in the war, both at home and abroad, the end of the conflict still left them second-class citizens, though their status had somewhat improved.

World War II

World War II created a series of circumstances that led many blacks to believe their long struggle for equality was nearly over. More than three million black Americans registered for the draft during World War II and nearly a million actually served in various branches of the armed forces. Lincoln University sent so many young men to the war that many people jokingly called the school a women's seminary during these years.

Black leaders demanded and succeeded in getting all branches of the armed services to accept Negroes. But only after a struggle and a threat by A. Phillip Randolph to lead a march on Washington. Black soldiers acquitted themselves well. Five American blacks received the Distinguished Service Cross and eighty-two black pilots received the Distinguished Flying Cross as a result of their gallantry during World War II. Perhaps Missouri's most famous black fighter was a former Lincoln student, St. Louisan Captain Wendell Pruitt, a member of the 99th Fighter Squadron who won many medals for his valor in Europe. Pruitt flew seventy missions in Italy and was credited with destroying eleven Nazi planes and sinking one destroyer. He was awarded the Distinguished Flying Cross and the air medal with seven Oak Leaf Clusters. Although Pruitt survived numerous dangerous missions in the European theater of war, ironically he died in a crash during a training flight soon after his return to the United States. Racial prejudice was an obstacle even for those who wanted to serve their country. An attempt by the air force to set up black military training programs at Jefferson Barracks in St. Louis was successfully opposed by whites in the city. The program had to be moved to Tuskegee Institute in Alabama instead.

The Effects of the War at Home. While the war raged in Europe and the Far East, blacks found new job opportunities at home. A process similar to the one that had accompanied World War I occurred: with immigration from overseas cut off and manpower shortages resulting from the draft, laborers were in great demand. Once again, blacks flooded the urban industrial centers to meet the need. By 1943, white St. Louisans complained that the demand for black laborers had made it almost impossible to find domestic workers.

It was the flood of black workers to northern cities that stimulated racial tensions. A serious race riot broke out in Detroit in June 1943. Many people in St. Louis braced for what they thought would be an equally serious outbreak in their own city. Bishop William Scarlett, head of the Episcopal Church of Missouri and president of the St. Louis Urban League, formed a committee to defuse racial tensions before they exploded. The Scarlett committee was a voluntary group of approximately twenty members, including business and professional people of both races, labor leaders, sociologists, elected officials, and public-spirited citizens generally. The committee worked with Governor Forrest Donnell, Mayor William D. Becker, and with police and army officials to prevent a duplication of the experience in Detroit. Although there were numerous minor racial conflicts, a major riot was avoided. Racial problems were only magnified when the war ended and American men returned home, flooding the job and housing markets.

Gardening at Cropperville colony, 1942. (*St. Louis Post-Dispatch*)

Main street in Cropperville colony, 1942. (*St. Louis Post-Dispatch*)

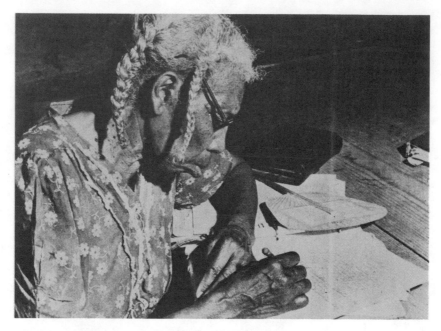

Mrs. Mary Gillian learning to write in a WPA supervised adult study group in Cropperville colony, 1942. (*St. Louis Post-Dispatch*)

Farming in the Cropperville colony, 1942. (*St. Louis Post-Dispatch*)

Political candidate speaking at Cropperville colony, 1943. (*St. Louis Post-Dispatch*)

The census of 1950 reflected the changes that had occurred during the war years. Missouri's population in 1950 was 3,954,653 of whom 2,954,653 were white and 297,000 were black. Although blacks constituted roughly 7.4 percent of the population, more than three-fourths (76.9 percent) of the blacks resided in the state's two metropolitan areas. Jackson County, which included Kansas City, had 57,043 blacks out of a total population of 541,032 (10.5 percent), while St. Louis and St. Louis County had 171,461 (13.6 percent) blacks out of a total population of 1,263,145. Within the city of St. Louis, the 154,448 blacks comprised 18 percent of the city's residents. The remainder of the black population was found chiefly in the southeastern counties of the Bootheel and along the Mississippi and Missouri rivers. In Mississippi County blacks constituted 21.8 percent of the inhabitants and in New Madrid County, 16 percent. The poverty of many of these rural blacks was graphically illustrated in the extremely poor black community of Cropperville, located about fifteen miles southwest of Poplar Bluff. Cropperville was "home" for about sixty-five black families who constituted the remnant of the fifteen hundred sharecroppers who had been evicted in 1939. Many residents still lived in tents the year round. Most of the wage earners in this colony worked as seasonal farmhands,

Night class conducted by teacher Whalen Ellison of Poplar Bluff in Cropper-ville colony, 1942. *(St. Louis Post-Dispatch)*

some going as far north as Michigan to pick fruit. Family income among Cropperville residents was extremely low, ranging from $35 to $195 per year. The average was only $50.

Persistent Segregation in Missouri

Discrimination in Employment. Once the war was over, former soldiers, now potential workers, rejoined the labor force and thus increased the competition for jobs. The blacks who found employment tended to occupy unskilled positions and perform domestic or menial tasks. Of the 109,024 blacks in the Missouri labor force in 1950, 59,081 (54 percent), were in service employments, while another 18,000 were common laborers. Only 23,305 were connected with industry, and most of them were in unskilled jobs. Black workers found promotions difficult to obtain and white collar jobs extremely rare. In general, they were also the first to be fired during slack times. The unemployment rate for blacks in St. Louis was estimated to be 15 percent in 1954, more than two and one-half times the rate for white workers. Not surprisingly, blacks who did find jobs made less money than

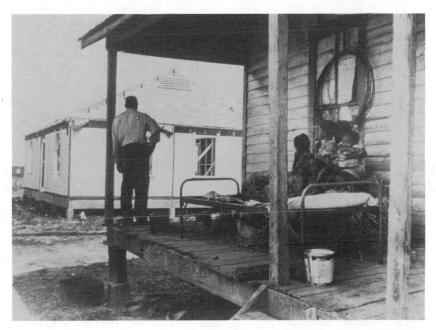

Home built by the Farm Security Administration for black sharecroppers in southeastern Missouri, 1941. (*Charles Trefts Collection, State Historical Society of Missouri*)

whites. In 1950 the gross average yearly income for black St. Louis workers was only 58 percent of that made by their white counterparts.

Housing. Because of low income, prejudice, or unemployment, housing was almost as critical a problem for blacks as job finding. Black neighborhoods were usually overcrowded and lacked adequate police protection, sanitation facilities, and other necessary services. They became fertile breeding places for crime, vice, and delinquency. Virtually every town in the state with a black population had its "Niggertown."

Housing restrictions and overcrowding were particulary evident in St. Louis. A subcommittee of the state's Advisory Committee on Civil Rights estimated in 1958 that although blacks comprised approximately 30 percent of the city's total population, only about 16-20 percent of the residential housing was available to them. New housing was particularly difficult for blacks to obtain. An estimated ninety-five thousand blacks moved to St. Louis between 1950 and 1957. Despite that huge number, less than one hundred new homes were built for them. A similar situation existed in Kansas City between 1940 and

1958; only 106 building permits were issued for new single-family black housing.

The explanation offered for the unfavorable housing condition of blacks in Missouri was the supposedly greater risk posed by the prospective black home buyer. It was harder for him to get credit because of his low employment and income status. When blacks could get loans, informal agreements by real estate dealers often made it difficult for willing white owners to sell to them in white neighborhoods.

Public Accommodations. Discrimination against blacks in places of public accommodation was general throughout Missouri during the period of the forties and into the fifties. Public facilities that whites took for granted were closed to blacks. It was difficult for blacks to find lodging in hotels, motels, or rooming houses. They could not eat in restaurants, cafeterias, snack bars, or roadside stands. Soda fountains, drug counters, ice cream parlors, and similar facilities refused them service. Even black businessmen, legislators, and members of the professions reported difficulty finding restroom facilities while traveling across the state. Blacks wishing to get a drink of water had to go through the humiliating experience of approaching the fountain marked "colored," and if they could find a white doctor or dentist to treat them, they had to wait in a separate Negro waiting room.

Discrimination also continued in recreational facilities, such as theaters, drive-ins, bowling alleys, skating rinks, swimming pools, and golf courses. Jefferson City, with only two "public" pools, maintained one for whites and one for blacks.

Challenges to Segregation

But if the forties and early fifties saw persistent segregation in the state of Missouri, they also witnessed successful challenges to the system. The liberal atmosphere resulting from the New Deal era and the judicial successes against discrimination of the thirties, when combined with the movement of blacks into new and higher paying jobs which resulted from World War II, spurred blacks to step up their challenges against the status quo. Progress came in a variety of areas.

As early as 1943, a Lincoln University Law School professor won a case which kept him from being forced out of his home in a white residential neighborhood in St. Louis. White groups, including the Market Avenue Protective Association and the St. Louis Real Estate Exchange, had attempted to bar Professor Scovel Richardson from his home on Market Street.

Desegregation of the Armed Forces. One of the most important federal challenges to segregation in the forties came at the hands of Missourian Harry S Truman, who succeeded to the presidency in 1945 following the sudden death of Franklin D. Roosevelt. It was President Truman who led the way in abolishing segregation in the armed forces. On July 26, 1948, Truman issued the following order:

> It is hereby declared to be the policy of the President that there shall be equality of treatment and opportunity for all persons in the armed services without regard to race, color, religion or national origin. This policy shall be put into effect as rapidly as possible, having due regard to the time required to effectuate any necessary changes without impairing efficiency or morale.

Truman also created a Committee on Equality of Treatment and Opportunity in the Armed Services to implement this order. Although the armed services dragged their feet in complying with Truman's order, by 1949 the army had at least officially opened all jobs to servicemen regardless of race and had abolished racial quotas. The navy and air force later followed suit. Thereafter, the military became one of the most important sources of vocational training and career employment for blacks, although some discrimination continued. As late as 1967, blacks made up only 5 percent of the army's eleven thousand officers.

Public Accommodations. Challenges to segregation also came in the area of public accommodations. A number of social organizations were active in promoting racial goodwill, among them the NAACP, the Urban League, the Missouri Association for Social Welfare, the League of Women Voters, the Catholic Interracial Conference, and the National Conference of Christians and Jews. Often these groups sponsored law suits against discriminatory agencies and institutions. Private individuals of both races and all faiths also joined the struggle for human rights.

Indeed, it was only through legal challenges to segregation that changes were made. It was, for example, court pressure which opened the public swimming pools to blacks in St. Louis and Kansas City in 1950 and 1953, respectively. These legal successes encouraged voluntary desegregation. After long negotiations by civil rights organizations the Jefferson Hotel of St. Louis opened its doors to blacks for the first time in 1952, and was followed shortly thereafter by several others. Two years later, some Kansas City hotels did likewise. A few restaurants in both cities began accepting black patrons, with railroad and airport facilities leading the way.

The greater concern of communities for improved race relations was shown by the establishment of official groups to improve interracial goodwill. Two municipal bodies of this nature were the St. Louis

Council on Human Relations, of which Chester Stovall was Executive Director, and the Kansas City Commission on Human Relations with William Gremley as Director. Jefferson City had, for a short time, a Mayor's Committee on Human Relations.

Churches. White churches generally continued to deny membership to blacks in the forties, although there were notable exceptions. The Catholic Church, in particular, took a strong stand in favor of integration. The movement toward integration was the result of a decade or more of prodding by St. Louis priests. Archbishop, and later Cardinal, John J. Glennon of St. Louis refused to follow the lead of the priests, however, largely because he feared alienating wealthy church supporters. It was left for his successor, Cardinal Joseph E. Ritter, to end segregation in 1947. Cardinal Ritter directed all pastors under his jurisdiction to carry out the following:

> . . .there should be no discrimination and. . .the same principles for admission are to be followed in admitting colored children as for others. This is in keeping with our Catholic teaching and the best principles of our American form of democratic government.

Churches of other denominations began slowly to open their doors to black membership.

The Crucial Challenge: Education

Perhaps the greatest challenge to segregation came in the area of education. Access to education had long been seen as the major vehicle for social progress. In the forties most black schools were still physically inferior to white facilities, often located in undesirable places, near taverns, or even houses of prostitution. The textbooks which were used, especially in rural districts, were often old, outdated castoffs from the white schools. The subjects which were taught and the facilities provided in white schools were frequently not offered in, or furnished for, black schools. Black teachers were poorly paid as compared to their white counterparts. Although in large urban communities the training of black teachers compared favorably with that of white teachers, in small urban and rural centers frequently the reverse was true. Many black and white rural teachers had only a high school diploma, or, at best, a two-year normal school certificate.

Black children, lacking schools in their own districts, were often transported long distances to schools in other towns. Fifty high school children from Fulton traveled twenty-five miles to the Laboratory High School in Jefferson City; Madison's eight black children, transported to Moberly, had to leave home an hour and a half before other children. Supervision in most black schools, moreover, was not as strict as in white schools. In short, separate schools for blacks usually meant inferior schools.

Even more disastrous was the effect of segregated schools upon the black child. It automatically branded him as inferior with the sanction of the law. It affected his aspirations, his motivation to learn, filled him with frustration, and made him regard himself as an "outsider." The opposite was true of the white child.

Blacks and the Universities. In Missouri, continual efforts were made after 1945 to open the University of Missouri to qualified black students. Leading the vanguard were the metropolitan newspapers of St. Louis, the *Post-Dispatch* and *Globe Democrat,* and of Kansas City, the *Times* and *Star,* as well as the black newspapers of those cities, whose editorials advocated integrating the university.

Student support at the University of Missouri also helped. Campus polls showed overwhelming support for immediate integration. Liberal faculty members at the university, in concert with colleagues from Lincoln University, lent their support. Likewise, individuals and organizations from throughout the state—lay, professional, and religious—swelled the ranks of those working for greater educational opportunities for blacks. Integration-minded groups sponsored legislation to eliminate segregation in education. Bills introduced by these organizations in the legislature were lost either in the House or the Senate, however.

In 1949, a bill to admit blacks to the University of Missouri when similar courses were not offered at Lincoln University was amended in the House to apply to all the state colleges. The House passed the bill by an overwhelming vote, but the Senate defeated it. Disillusioned by the failure of the legislature to open the university to all qualified students, three seniors at Lincoln University applied for admission to the Graduate School at Columbia, and the School of Mines and Metallurgy at Rolla in the spring of 1950. Elmer Bell, George Everett Horne, and Gus T. Ridgel applied, believing that they would be admitted, should a court case be necessary. The Board of Curators of the University of Missouri sought a ruling from the Circuit Court of Cole County. In a crowded courtroom on June 27, 1950, Judge Sam Blair ordered the students admitted forthwith to the University of Missouri. They were duly enrolled at the University in September 1950, along with several other blacks. All were well received. Thus, after more than a century of segregation, the doors of the University of Missouri were finally opened to black students.

Other Public Schools. With the walls of the university breached, efforts between 1950 and 1954 centered on opening other public educational facilities. Between 1950 and 1954, four attempts were made by blacks in St. Louis, St. Louis County, and Kansas City, to enroll in white schools. In *State ex rel Toliver* v. *Board of Education of the City of St. Louis,* a black student at Stowe Teachers College applied for admission to the white Harris Teachers College. The application was denied. The student then sought a court order to compel Harris Teachers College to admit him. The applicant contended that substantial inequalities existed between Stowe and Harris colleges, in the accreditation granted to the two schools, the inequality of the faculties, the libraries, and the laboratories. The plea was denied on the ground that substantially equal privileges and facilities existed.

More successful was a black student at the Washington Technical High School for Negroes in St. Louis, who in the same year applied for permission to enroll at Hadley Technical High School. Hadley Tech was for white students only. When his application was rejected, the black student tried unsuccessfully to get the Board of Education of St. Louis to set up an identical course at Washington Technical High School. The board refused the request, stating that such a course could not be offered unless ten students were enrolled. The student then filed suit against the Board of Education. The Appellate Court decided in favor of the student and ordered him to be enrolled in the course. Hadley Tech dropped the course, however, rather than admit a black student. White students therefore suffered deprivation of instruction as well as blacks so that segregation could be maintained.

With this case as a precedent, 150 black students in Kansas City attempted to integrate a school for whites which had an auditorium and a gymnasium. These facilities, the defendants argued, were essential to education in the modern era. The court denied the appeal on the grounds that sufficient evidence had not been produced to substantiate the appellant's plea. The record cited by the court showed nineteen schools without auditoriums and ten without gymnasiums. Although the court held it did not discount the importance of gymnasiums and auditoriums in the total educational program, the law required substantial equality. Such equality was not denied when facilities were not identical. The guarantee was for *substantially* equal educational opportunities; difference in the physical plant, therefore, was not inequality.

Obviously, because of the peculiar interpretation of the courts, the "separate but equal" doctrine was difficult and expensive to challenge successfully. Nevertheless, interested persons noted a changing attitude by federal appellate courts to segregation cases. The result was a direct attack upon the equal but separate doctrine.

This occurred in 1954 when, in *Arnold* v. *Kirkwood School District R-7*, a black student tried to attend a white school in his district. Equality of opportunity and faculties were conceded. The only contention was the illegality of separateness. Denied in the Federal District Court, the plaintiff appealed to the United States Court of Appeals. After hearing arguments, the latter tribunal decided to withhold judgment. The Supreme Court of the United States was expected shortly to decide five education cases before it and the Circuit Court elected to wait and be governed by the higher court's decision. On May 17, 1954, the United States Supreme Court handed down its long-awaited decision in *Brown* v. *Board of Education of Topeka, Kansas*, holding that racial segregation in public education was unconstitutional. Thus, fifty-eight years after the Supreme Court put its stamp of approval upon segregation in *Plessy* v. *Ferguson*, an enlightened judiciary struck down the constitutional and legal basis for racial discrimination in education in seventeen states and the District of Columbia. Missouri was one of these states.

Individual Black Successes

Perhaps just as important during these years was the fact that numerous blacks in all walks of life were rising to positions of achievement and success, despite discrimination. They were therefore able to offer black youth positive role models, while illustrating to whites the absurdity of racial stereotypes. Early examples of Missouri blacks who made outstanding contributions included Clarence Gregg, known for his machine gun and smoke-consuming devices; John McClennand for sparktimers, oil pumps, and carburetors; and Robert H. Pennington for his railroad signals.

Oscar S. Ficklin was the first black chemist to work for the Union Electric Company in St. Louis. He had gone to work as a porter for the company in 1905. Later, after completing correspondence courses in chemistry through a school in Scranton, Pennsylvania in 1920, he was promoted to chemist in charge of the testing laboratory, a position he held for nearly a quarter of a century. In 1945 he became the first black person to be named foreman of a court jury, having been elected by his eleven white counterparts.

In 1956, Theodore McMillian became the first black in Missouri appointed to a circuit judgeship. McMillian, a black from St. Louis who was educated at Lincoln University, received a law degree from St. Louis University. He served as an Assistant Circuit Attorney and earned a reputation as a brilliant trial lawyer. On October 2, 1978, he was sworn in as a judge of the federal appeals court.

Josephine Baker, international entertainer.
(*St. Louis American*)

Elmer Simms Campbell, a native St. Louisan, had become an internationally acclaimed illustrator and commercial artist by the forties. *Esquire* magazine featured his work from its beginning in 1933. James D. Parks had begun a career in art which led to subsequent international recognition. James W. Spaulding of Kansas City went to work as a porter for the City National Bank of Kansas City in 1919. He stayed with the bank for more than thirty years, later rising to the position of Superintendent of Records and Supplies.

In the forties Chauncy Downs replaced Count Basie as the leading jazz figure in Kansas City. Running a close second to Downs was the legendary alto saxophonist Charlie (Yardbird) Parker, who died in 1955 at the young age of thirty-five. On the stage, Josephine Baker, born in St. Louis in 1907, became an international celebrity, and Etta Moton gained fame as a singer.

The 1940s also saw the passing of one of Missouri's most famous

Dr. George Washington Carver at work in his laboratory. (*George Washington Carver Museum, Tuskegee Institute*)

black geniuses, George Washington Carver. Carver was born a slave near Diamond Grove, Missouri, during the Civil War. He later gained fame at Tuskegee Institute, Alabama, for his research with sweet potatoes, peanuts, cotton, soybeans, and wood. His discoveries revolutionized southern agriculture. On July 14, 1943, the 210-acre farm on which he was born was dedicated as a national monument under the supervision of the National Park Service.

In 1945, Dr. J. C. Castron became the first black member of St. Louis' Board of Aldermen. William A. Massingale of St. Louis was elected to the General Assembly in 1946. Massingale was joined in 1948 by prominent Kansas City pharmacologist J. McKinley Neal. Neal was only the second Kansas City black to serve in the legislature. He followed L. A. Knox, dean of Kansas City's black lawyers, who was elected in the late twenties. Newspaper reporter Lester Walton of St. Louis served as United States minister to Liberia from 1935 to 1945. In 1954 President Dwight D. Eisenhower named Jesse Ernest Wilkins of Farmington as an Assistant Secretary of Labor.

Missouri's most accomplished black writer, Langston Hughes, had reached the apex of his career by the forties. He gained fame during the Harlem Renaissance of the twenties, and in 1930 he wrote a widely acclaimed novel entitled *Not Without Laughter* and produced in 1934 a volume of short stories, *The Ways of White Folks*. Later, he produced a number of plays, the most famous of which was *Mulatto*.

Three black Missouri newspapers were also going strong in the forties: the *Kansas City Call*, founded by Chester A. Franklin in 1919; the *St. Louis Argus*, founded in 1912 by J. E. Mitchell, Sr.; and the *St. Louis American*, established in 1928 by Nathaniel Sweets. These newspapers provided a forum for discussion of issues of particular importance to blacks, as well as a source of racial identity and accomplishment. They were supplemented by the work of the YMCAs and YWCAs of Kansas City and St. Louis. Mrs. Elsie Mountain of Kansas City was particularly effective in preparing girls for jobs which ordinarily they could not have obtained. Ms. Anna Lee Hill Scott performed the same service in St. Louis.

Segregation *was* being challenged successfully, in both the state and the nation. Moreover, individual blacks were achieving success in American society, in spite of persistent racial barriers. An optimism began to crop up among blacks in the state. Hope—as real and intense as the hope born during the Civil War—was again the watchword for black life in Missouri.

SUGGESTED READINGS

The best general account of the black soldier in World War II is Ulysses Lee, *The Employment of Negro Troops*, (Washington, 1967). Richard M. Dalfiume, *Desegregation of the U.S. Armed Forces: Fighting on Two Fronts, 1939-1953*, (Columbia, 1969) is an authoritative study of the efforts to integrate the military. The relationship between Missourian Harry Truman and black Americans is discussed in Philip H. Vaughan, "The Truman Administration's Fair Deal for Black Americans," *Missouri Historical Review*, LXX (April 1976), pages 291-305.

The early efforts of the Catholic church to desegregate in St. Louis are covered in Donald J. Kempker, "Catholic Integration in St. Louis, 1935-1947," *Missouri Historical Review*, LXXIII (October 1978), pages 1-22. The best overall treatment of the status of Negro education and general social conditions before the decision in 1954 *Brown v. Board of Education of Topeka, Kansas* is Lorenzo J. Greene, *Desegregation of Schools in Missouri* (Jefferson City, 1959). An excellent examination of black civil rights in Missouri before and after 1954 is Thomas E. Baker, "Human Rights in Missouri," Ph.D. thesis, (University of Missouri—Columbia, 1975). Baker's thesis may be ordered directly from University Microfilms International, 300 N. Zeeb Road, Ann Arbor, MI 48106.

10

Free at Last?
From Civil Rights to Black Power
1954-1968

May 17, 1954, was a day of rejoicing for black Americans and their liberal white allies. On this day the United States Supreme Court unanimously decreed that segregation in public schools was a violation of the equal protection clause of the Fourteenth Amendment and therefore unconstitutional. Speaking for the full Court, Chief Justice Warren said in part that to separate black children

> from others of similar age and qualifications solely because of their race generates a feeling of inferiority as to their status in the community that may affect their hearts and minds in a way unlikely to be undone. . . . We conclude that in the field of public education the doctrine of "separate but equal" has no place. Separate educational facilities are inherently unequal.

This famous case of *Brown* v. *Board of Education of Topeka, Kansas* took its name from Linda Carol Brown, whose father tired of seeing his daughter denied access to a nearby white school and challenged the constitutionality of the Kansas law which separated white and black students. The result was perhaps the most important decision handed down by the Supreme Court in the twentieth century. Most black Americans hailed the decision as the dawn of a new era. At last, they believed, they had the key to full citizenship. Black Americans would apply this new doctrine to all phases of American life. Once segregation in education had been declared in violation of the Constitution, they reasoned, they could no longer be denied all other benefits of American society solely on the basis of their skin color.

The Brown Decision and Missouri

The decision caused mixed reactions throughout the nation. It brought forth angry responses in the deep South. Elsewhere, there was less resistance. In the northern and border states many whites joined with blacks in praising the decision. In Missouri, the State Commission of Education asked the Attorney General what effect the Brown case would have on the state's racially segregated schools. In June 1954, he responded that Missouri's school segregation laws were null and void. Integration, as the Supreme Court ordered the next year, must proceed "with all deliberate speed."

Although Missouri generally escaped the determined and violent opposition to integration that later occurred in the South, the process in Missouri was not without its difficulties. Most school districts in the state agreed to submit desegregation plans. There were notable exceptions, however, particularly in the Bootheel, or southeastern, section of the state. Charleston, for example, made determined efforts to avoid any form of school desegregation into the middle of the 1960s. In other parts of the Bootheel as late as the mid-sixties, black children still went to school in the summer to make up for a two-month cotton-picking recess in the fall. In addition, despite the Supreme Court ruling, many black pupils still traveled as far as thirty-five miles, past all-white schools, to attend black schools in dilapidated sections of small agricultural towns. Many libraries, parks, theaters, and other recreational facilities also remained closed to blacks. In some southeastern and mid-Missouri communities, blacks were still required to sit behind a rope, in an all-black section, at movie houses.

Black teachers often became expendable because of desegregation. In Malden, Potosi, Lexington, Jefferson City, Clinton, Henrietta, and other communities, black teachers lost their jobs. The total number ranged from between 125 and 150. Eleven teachers lost their jobs in Moberly when desegregation took place in 1955. They sued the school board but lost their case.

Desegregation got off to a better start in St. Louis and Kansas City where 90 percent of the state's black school-age children lived. The major problem with implementing the Brown decision there was that blacks were segregated into all-black neighborhoods. Integration of the school district meant little if the district itself was virtually all black. Consequently, by the 1960s, even though most Missouri school districts were legally desegregated, most black students were still attending all-black schools.

One way to address this form of segregation was to bus students from one district into another. But when school districts turned to busing students to achieve racial integration difficulties appeared. The process that occurred in St. Louis illustrates the point. During the school year 1961-1962, the St. Louis school board decided that pupils to be bused would come from predominately or all-black schools. The twenty schools receiving the bused students were all-white, and 95 percent of the bused pupils were black. The students were bused as entire classes rather than as individuals, so that while a school building might be integrated, classrooms remained segregated. Indeed, many of the transported students had little contact with pupils who lived in the receiving districts. In some schools blacks and whites ate at different times. They also were restricted to separate parts of the playgrounds. In 1961-1962, some 4,653 black students were transported from the overcrowded schools of St. Louis' West End. The following school year about 6,000 students, mostly black, were bused. However, the segregated housing situation nullified any real efforts at successful integration. By 1965, 91 percent of the black elementary school children in St. Louis attended all-black or predominately black schools. In 1966, nearly 40 percent of Missouri's black schoolchildren were in schools that were at least 95 percent black and 35 percent of the black pupils were in all-black schools.

Human Rights

The Human Rights Commission. The more basic problem, of course, was housing, and the fact that black people were not free to choose where they lived. Housing, in turn, was at least partly dependent upon income and jobs; black people who were occupationally discriminated against on the basis of race found it difficult to move out of the ghetto. Increasingly, therefore, it became apparent that the fight against segregation was a complicated, many-pronged affair. A more organized effort was needed.

Many Missourians looked for the state to lead the way in fighting discrimination. Social welfare groups and interested individuals reasoned that if segregation and discrimination were to be combated successfully, the majesty of the state's laws had to be invoked. In 1954, liberal organizations such as the NAACP, the Missouri Association for Social Welfare, the National Association of Christians and Jews, the Urban League, and the National Catholic Conference persuaded a bi-partisan group of senators and representatives to back the introduction

of a bill calling for a human rights commission. Furthermore, they secured a promise from the governor-elect, James T. Blair, that he would
support such a bill. Although opposition to the bill delayed its passage,
it finally became law in mid-1957. At last the state of Missouri recognized that the deprivation of rights on the basis of race was the state's
official concern.

The new Human Rights Commission did not change race relations
in Missouri overnight. With a limited budget and little power, about all
it could do was to point out the reality of discrimination in Missouri
and encourage individuals who were discriminated against to file
charges. But that alone would prove to be helpful. What was the
situation that the newly-formed Human Rights Commission faced and
what kind of progress was made toward integration in the fifties and
sixties? Those questions can be answered best by looking at the status
of blacks in the state in several categories during that time period.

Housing. Much of the housing market was still closed to blacks in the
mid-fifties. A majority of St. Louis realtors, for example, were still in
favor of blacks being permitted to buy housing only in restricted
"Negro districts." The Commission on Human Rights conducted a survey in 1960 and found residential segregation widespread in nearly
every part of the state. Some areas of the state excluded blacks alto-
gether. They maintained "sundown laws," that is, no blacks were permitted to stay in town after sunset. One northwest Missouri township
advertised that it had a "nigger free" work force for any new industries.

The federal government tried to solve at least some of the housing
problems by erecting public housing projects in the inner cities. Unfortunately, these well-intentioned efforts were often poorly planned,
taking little note of the human needs of the projects' residents. The
classic example of the government's failure in this regard was the
Pruitt-Igoe Housing Project near downtown St. Louis. Begun in the
early fifties, and first occupied in 1954, Pruitt-Igoe was an all-black
project containing thirty-three eleven-story buildings with 2,762 apartments and 10,000 residents. The buildings were poorly planned—their
elevators stopped only on the fourth, seventh, and tenth floors—and
they quickly became centers of crime and vice. By the seventies, the
government admitted its failure and destroyed all of the buildings in
the complex.

In June 1963, the Missouri Advisory Committee to the United States
Commission on Civil Rights reported discriminatory practices in hous-
ing in several Missouri communities including Mexico, St. Joseph,
Poplar Bluff, Kansas City, Charleston, St. Louis, and the counties of
Mississippi, Pemiscot, New Madrid, Cape Girardeau, and Clay. In the

PERCENT OF NONWHITE POPULATION, 1960

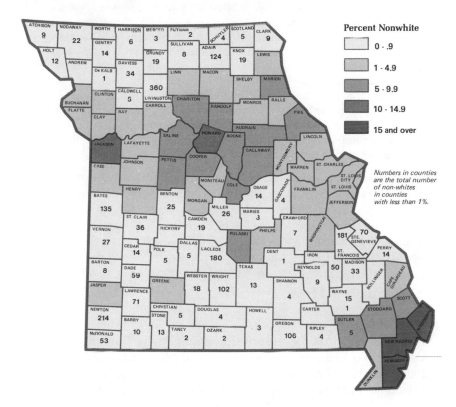

Percent Nonwhite

☐ 0 - .9

▨ 1 - 4.9

▨ 5 - 9.9

▨ 10 - 14.9

■ 15 and over

Numbers in counties are the total number of non-whites in counties with less than 1%.

late 1960s, 18 percent of all black housing in St. Louis was overcrowded, compared with 10 percent for the rest of the city. In Kansas City the figures were similar with nearly 10 percent of the housing in the non-white area overcrowded, compared with 5 percent for the rest of the city. Missourians would have to wait until the decade of the seventies for a statewide fair housing law.

Public Accommodations. Things were little better in the area of public accommodations. In 1949, the Missouri Association for Social Welfare had conducted a survey on discrimination in public facilities in the state. The investigators found that ". . . there are very few places in Missouri where a Negro can get overnight accommodations at a respectable hotel or eat in a first class restaurant." Ten years later, the Human Rights Commission found that there had been little or no improvement. The commission drew the following conclusion:

Negroes are prohibited from using the eating and sleeping accommodations in the majority of Missouri's hotels, motels, resorts,
restaurants, dining rooms, cafes, soda fountains, drugstores and
department store eating facilities. . . . In most cases in Missouri a
Negro may order food to "take out," but he is refused permission
to eat on the premises. In a number of counties, a Negro can be
served food in the kitchen, a back room, or in a screened-off
area. . . . A Negro can actually travel the width or breadth of the
state and not find one cafe, restaurant, hotel, motel or resort that
will accommodate him. Even when traveling on an interstate bus
in the uniform of his country, the Negro is often refused service at
the bus station rest stops.

Missouri blacks suffered humiliation and indignity for many more
years before discrimination in public accommodation was made illegal. It took several years of lobbying by groups such as the NAACP,
MASW, the Urban League, and the Human Rights Commission before a
reluctant legislature passed into law the Missouri Public Accommodation Act of 1965. Indeed, that act was passed in large part because the
state was being threatened by federal intervention if it failed to end
discrimination in public facilities.

Employment

Private Sector. In 1960 a study by the Human Rights Commission found
that even in the large metropolitan areas like St. Louis and Kansas City
"the great mass of Negro workers remains on the lowest levels of employment." In St. Louis, more than 10 percent of all nonwhite males in
the labor force were unemployed compared with 2.8 percent of white
males. Blacks were also confined mainly to the lowest paying jobs. An
examination of all industries revealed that 22 percent of white male
laborers were craftsmen, foremen, or kindred workers; only 8 percent of the black males were so employed. While only 5 percent of the
whites were employed as common laborers, 21 percent of the blacks
fell into that category. Only 3 percent of the black males in the labor
force were classified as professionals, compared to 11 percent of the
white males. In other parts of the state the situation was often worse.
The Missouri Advisory Committee to the United States Commission on
Civil Rights reported in 1963 that employment discrimination existed
throughout the state. Referring to the employment situation in Mexico
(Audrain County) the report stated:

The economy of the Negro community is kept at a substandard
level as a consequence of Negroes being restricted to menial and
low salaried jobs. Their range of occupations is narrowed down to
custodial or janitorial workers in stores, factories, and offices;
domestic and janitorial workers in the City Hall and Court House;

cooks and waiters at the Missouri Military Academy, and small businesses in the Negro ghetto. . . . Negroes are not employed in the construction of urban renewal projects because they must belong to unions.

The report found similar conditions existing in St. Joseph, Poplar Bluff, Jackson, Clay, and Platte counties, and throughout Southeast Missouri. In St. Joseph the attitude of many members of the business community was expressed by one businessman who publicly complained to a fellow businessman, who had recently hired a black clerical worker, "Well, you're starting a precedent now. All the white businessmen in St. Joe are going to have to put nigger gals in their offices."

In Poplar Bluff there was equally widespread discrimination in employment. Two blacks were employed as janitors at the court house. Some blacks were employed at car lots and garages "as flunkies." At the three local hospitals, many blacks were employed mainly as maids and dishwashers; there were a few black nurses. One black was employed at the local box factory. There were no blacks employed by the Missouri Highway Maintenance Department and the shoe and garment factories of Poplar Bluff.

In largely agricultural southeastern Missouri employment discrimination was perhaps the worst in the state. Here even the traditional menial jobs reserved for blacks in other parts of the state were held by whites. The economic situation of the black population of Charleston was such that approximately 50 percent of the black people there could not afford housing with running water or modern bathroom facilities.

On the bright side of the employment picture, professional sports were finally being integrated. As early as the late nineteenth century, Tom Bass distinguished himself as a jockey and horse trainer. Since that time black Missourians have contributed to many sports. In 1947 the Brooklyn Dodgers' Jackie Robinson broke the color line banning black baseball players in the major leagues. Robinson's presence in the big leagues paved the way for scores of athletes in all sports. In Missouri, it meant that longtime players in the all-Negro leagues, such as the legendary Satchel Paige, would have the opportunity to play major league ball. Had it not been for Robinson, the outstanding careers of St. Louis Cardinals Bob Gibson and Lou Brock, as well as a host of other black athletes, might never have been allowed to contribute to the richness of the state's athletic tradition. Presently Missouri's blacks are participants in professional baseball, basketball, football, and boxing.

Public Employment. There was as much discrimination in employ-

Satchel Paige during his days
with the St. Louis Browns.
(St. Louis Post-Dispatch)

St. Louis Cardinal Lou Brock and former Cardinal pitcher Bob Gibson. *(St. Louis Post-Dispatch)*

ment in the public sector as in private business. In 1963, the Human Rights Commission conducted a survey on black employment in state agencies. Although the percentage of black state employees nearly equalled their percentage of the general population, blacks were mostly employed in janitorial, maintenance, and other menial jobs. Access to professional, technical, and even clerical jobs was largely denied them. Blacks constituted a little less than 8 percent of the state employees, but only about 2 percent of them earned over four thousand dollars a year. Many of the largest state agencies had few black employees. This was particularly true of the Highway Patrol, the Highway Department, the Conservation Department, the Department of Corrections, the Division of Health, and all the state colleges, except, of course, Lincoln University.

There was little improvement in the situation by 1968, when the commission conducted another survey. Blacks represented a little over 9 percent of the state workers. Yet widespread discrimination in employment opportunities kept them disproportionately confined to the lowest paying jobs. While more than 70 percent of black state employees earned less than four hundred dollars a month, only 35 percent of the white state employees earned so little. The percentage of blacks employed varied from agency to agency. The Missouri Highway Patrol employed only 13 blacks out of a work force of 1294 employees, less than one percent. Similarly, the State Highway Department had only 33 black workers out of a total work force of 5,768 employees. Both agencies attempted greater efforts in minority employment after 1968.

Organized Black Protest

Nonviolence: Boycotts and Sit-ins. The slowness of progress in the face of the great promise of *Brown v. Board of Education* emboldened blacks to push more forcefully for an equal share of the rights of American citizenship. The decade of the sixties witnessed organized black protests such as the state and nation had never seen before. In both Kansas City and St. Louis, banks and stores that refused to hire blacks in other than menial positions were boycotted. Since blacks comprised nearly two-thirds of the unemployed in the St. Louis area in 1963, they felt that such an act was justified.

As early as 1960, Jefferson City, St. Louis, and Kansas City opened their restaurants to all segments of the public. That happened, however, only after organized demonstrations against a number of restaurants practicing discrimination, particularly in the two larger cities. In 1963, one Kansas City cafe owner who had operated at the same location for forty-three years still refused to serve blacks. A black sit-in forced him to close the establishment. It never reopened. In Jefferson

Reverend Jessie Jackson leading a protest march. (*St. Louis American*)

City, sit-ins and threatened boycotts by Lincoln University students forced city entrepreneurs to open their restaurants. At one time, Jefferson City's undefeated senior high school football team, after winning a hard fought struggle, stopped with its component of victorious whites and blacks at a restaurant on Madison Street to buy hamburgers and cokes. When the restaurant owner refused to serve the blacks, the whites ordered cokes and hamburgers. After the food was prepared, however, the white students refused to eat it or pay, telling the proprietor that they wanted no part of an eating establishment that would not serve blacks. They then went out and sat in silent protest on a curb in front of the restaurant.

Much of this strategy of boycotting and sitting-in was modeled after the behavior of national black leader Martin Luther King, Jr., chairman of the Southern Christian Leadership Conference. Advocating a nonviolent but persistent insistence on black equality, King organized protests throughout the South. His strategy called worldwide attention to the plight of black people and prompted the nation's leaders to outlaw segregation.

Federal Legislation. The most effective response to organized black

Dick Gregory returns to native Missouri
for rally. (*St. Louis American*)

protests was at the federal level. In 1964, under President Lyndon B.
Johnson's leadership, Congress enacted a Public Accommodations Act
which prohibited discrimination in all restaurants, theaters, stores,
parks, and other places generally open to the public. Getting a law
passed, however, was one thing and enforcing it quite another. In Kansas City, for example, a local judge temporarily restrained the imple-
mentation of the law on the grounds that it would cause too many
problems. Nevertheless the action on the federal level meant that battles for these rights would not have to be fought by blacks in all the
individual states.

The Public Accommodations Act of 1964 was followed by the
Voting Rights Act in 1965. It opened the way for hundreds of thousands of blacks to use the franchise more freely than they had ever
done before. Although blacks had had the right to vote since the adoption of the Fifteenth Amendment in 1870, the South had denied them
the ballot. The Civil Rights Acts of 1964 and 1965 inspired a new
confidence, prompting blacks to turn out in great numbers for candidates who promised to support the black struggle for equality. Just
how important that could be was made evident in the election of 1964
when black voters defied ward leaders in Kansas City to support the

ACTION, black militant group carrying "The Black Madonna." *(St. Louis American)*

reelection of United States Representative Richard Bolling. Freedom, Inc., a black political organization, led the pro–Bolling fight, arguing that the congressman's strong civil rights record and support for medical care for the aged entitled him to renomination.

Despite the gains, however, the status of the black masses was still very little improved. The opening up of white colleges and universities and the right to frequent hotels and restaurants were relatively unimportant to blacks who could not afford to take advantage of their new liberties. Black unemployment remained high, housing poor, and the general quality of life low. Many blacks argued that not enough was being done to end discrimination. The nonviolent and patient protesting of leaders such as King came under fire as a new contingent of black leaders began to emerge.

Black Militancy and Black Power. Gradually black militants came to exercise more and more influence in the civil rights movement. Malcolm X, Stokely Carmichael, H. Rap Brown, and others, began to advocate a violent confrontation with white society and about "black

During rally after the killing of Dr. King. (*St. Louis American*)

Memorial march honoring assassinated civil rights leader Dr. Martin Luther King, Jr. (*St. Louis American*)

Lincoln University campus disturbance in 1969. Jefferson City Mayor John Christy talks with student leaders. *(St. Louis American)*

power." This slogan was difficult to define. To some it meant black nationalism, to others black political power or a separate black economy and, to still others, it meant a third world made up of like-thinking persons of all races, creeds, and nationalities.

To most people involved in the movement, however, it meant a new sense of pride in the black past. Africa, rather than America, was defined as the black man's homeland. The word "Negro" was replaced by "black." Often these blacks shunned Christianity as the "white man's religion" and turned instead to the Nation of Islam, a religion founded in the 1930s by Elijah Muhammad. Many black Americans changed their names to African or Arabic ones and donned African dress. Black males and females changed their hair-styles. They read about their heritage, both in the United States and in Africa. The more they learned, the more they identified themselves as an oppressed people whose liberty could be gained only by revolutionary struggle.

The black power movement had both its advocates and critics. Both sides had to admit, however, that it caused the masses of blacks to become more active in the civil rights movement than they had ever been before. Black militants refused to associate with moderate blacks, decided that they could do without the monetary assistance of the white man, and clamored for black control of the ghetto and its institutions. They scoffed at King's direct nonviolent action. Instead, they called for black unity as a separate group and direct confrontation with the white man.

Violence. This hardened line met with an equally hard response; perhaps violence and bloodshed were inevitable. The years 1967 and 1968 saw riots all over the country. Beginning with the Watts district of Los Angeles in 1965, blacks pillaged and burned businesses in the ghetto. Missouri remained relatively quiet until the death of Martin Luther King in 1968. To most blacks, King's death signaled the killing of a dream. Frustration and anger turned to violence all over the country. When a local newspaper in Jefferson City ran a syndicated column the day before King was assassinated, branding him as a Communist, Lincoln students staged what was to have been a peaceful march to the newspaper office. After being told by the editor that the column could not be rescinded and that no apology would be forthcoming, the students responded with violence.

The Jefferson City incident was indeed minor compared with what occurred in Kansas City in 1968. The protest started because city officials refused to close schools in honor of the death of Martin Luther King. This angered Kansas City's black students, particularly since schools across the river, in Kansas City, Kansas, had been closed. Approximately three hundred black students marched to city hall to confront the mayor and demand the closing of the schools. The gathering was dispersed by police with tear gas. Later the same day, five all-black schools were closed after the police used tear gas against students milling about outside Lincoln High School. The students were forced into the school and then driven out again when police fired more tear gas into the building.

At dusk the first outbreaks began. Carloads of blacks were reported throwing molotov cocktails at police. Police Chief Clarence M. Kelley immediately authorized police to shoot any firebombers. Authorities called out the entire 900-man police force, 1700 National Guardsmen, and 168 state troopers to end the disturbance. On the first day of rioting two persons were killed, 44 injured and 175 arrested. The next day saw increased violence. Five persons were killed, all of them black civilians. At least ten persons were wounded as police and National Guardsmen exchanged fire with snipers.

The National Guard force was increased to 2,200 and an additional 700 troopers were rushed by Governor Warren E. Hearnes from central

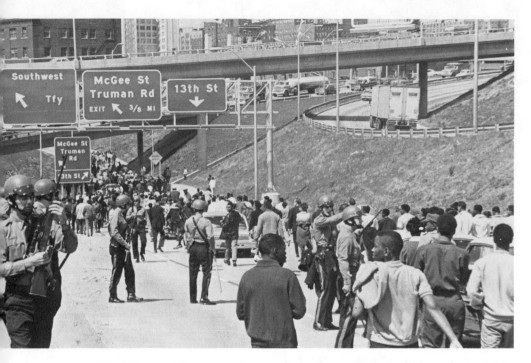

Black demonstrators marching in Kansas City. *(Kansas City Star)*

and eastern Missouri to Kansas City. During the evening 60 persons
were arrested and 57 injured, seven wounded by gunfire. Windows
were broken in over 200 businesses and 75 fires were started. The evening ended with more than 275 persons arrested. Most of the damage
was in the black sector. Later, some public officials admitted that law
enforcement personnel may have overreacted to the situation.

Moderation and Political Gains. In St. Louis too there were protests, but
with fewer incidences of violence. Too little time has passed to allow
for a full explanation of why Kansas City experienced such violence
and St. Louis did not. At least part of the answer, however, seems to lie
in the fact that many blacks in St. Louis felt that they had a greater part
to play in decision-making than their counterparts across the state. Although there were advocates of violence in St. Louis, more moderate
voices won out. It had helped that blacks had been elected to city-wide
positions during the late fifties and early sixties. In 1959, the Rev. John
J. Hicks became the first black to win a city-wide election in St. Louis
when he was chosen to serve on the school board. Of his election, Hicks

Five men arrested in Kansas City for violating the curfew. *(Kansas City Star)*

noted that "there had been apathy, a lethargy on their [blacks'] part for some time concerning things political, especially relating to the total life of the city." Likewise, in 1961 Chester E. Stovall became St. Louis' Director of Welfare, the city's first black person in that position and the first black to hold a cabinet-level job there.

Violence had mixed effects. On the one hand, it called attention to the grievances of blacks in the ghettoes. Blacks demanded jobs, better housing, health services, better police protection, and an end to police brutality. It opened up new opportunities in employment, politics, education, and health services. On the other hand, since most violence occurred in black neighborhoods, it left even more blacks homeless and jobless. But it was not meant to be a logical response to problems. Rather, it was an emotional rejoinder to frustration and disappointment. The fifties had started on such a positive note. The Brown decision in 1954 seemed to be the answer to the collective prayer of millions of black Americans. The successes of Martin Luther King and the verbal commitments to racial equality by Presidents Kennedy and Johnson further nurtured the dream. Black people's expectations were raised so high; in return, they got so little. Many wondered: could the dream be revived, in spite of the violence, and in spite of King's assassination?

SUGGESTED READINGS

Two works earlier mentioned are also useful in explaining the efforts of Missouri blacks to secure equality of education and first-class citizenship after 1954. For the successes and failures of school deseg-regation in Missouri until 1959, Lorenzo J. Greene, *Desegregation of Schools in Missouri* (Jefferson City, 1959), is an authoritative study. Thomas E. Baker's doctoral thesis, "Human Rights in Missouri" (University of Missouri-Columbia, 1975), provides an excellent overview of the Afro-American struggle for first-class citizenship in Missouri and an inside view of the advances and shortcomings of the Missouri Commission on Human Rights during its first fifteen years.

The Missouri Commission on Human Rights' *Study of Human Rights in Missouri, 1960* (Jefferson City, 1960), shows the lack of progress in the area of human rights in Missouri to that late date. The Missouri Advisory Committee to the U.S. Civil Rights Commission, *Report* (Jefferson City, 1963), provides much evidence of the continuation of discrimination in outstate Missouri and the two major urban areas—Kansas City and St. Louis. Rex Campbell and Peter C. Robertson, *The Negro in Missouri, 1960* (Jefferson City, 1967), is a compilation of useful statistical data from the U.S. Census of 1960.

We Shall Overcome:
The Struggle Goes On

The assassination of Martin Luther King, Jr., and the violent response that it evoked among blacks, occurred in a year filled with momentous events, the implications of which may not be fully understood for years to come. Perhaps the best we can do at this point is simply describe what happened; understanding will come later.

Conservatism and Realism

For many young black Americans, King's assassination was the last straw. They had seen their leaders—Medgar Evers, Malcolm X, and Martin Luther King, Jr.—killed off. Their disillusionment and frustration turned to anger and violence. Social justice, which had seemingly been the goal of the sixties, gave way to a white backlash. When Robert F. Kennedy was murdered in June of 1968, American idealism and the hope of social justice were shattered. Many Americans were fearful of the future.

Law and Order. Conservative whites turned to Richard M. Nixon. Nixon did not create a new mood in the country so much as he tapped and nurtured a sentiment that already existed. Americans, and among them Missourians, were tired—tired of the rapid social changes of the sixties, tired of violence, tired of fighting a losing war in Vietnam, simply tired of confusion and anxiety. They blamed most of the problems of the sixties on an idealism that they thought was simply unworkable. Therefore, they began to concern themselves more with their individual problems than with the social aspirations of less fortunate members of society.

Richard Nixon interpreted his election as a mandate to reverse the liberal trends of the fifties and sixties. He believed that Americans were becoming less willing to pour money into a war on poverty whose end was nowhere in sight. Predictably, federal funds for the poor, a disproportionate number of whom were black, began to dry up. It became increasingly difficult to pass programs with funds for health, education, and welfare, and once again the nation's deprived citizens were forced to fend for themselves.

Inflation and Affirmative Action. As if things were not bad enough, the decade of the seventies saw Americans confronted by economic problems that puzzled even the experts. Runaway inflation of 10 percent or more a year threatened to lower the living standards of even middle-class citizens; to the poor and aged, many of whom were on fixed incomes, it was disastrous. The long-held American dream that each generation of American citizens would live better than its parents was jeopardized. The poor and many blacks in the nation's cities gave up hope of moving ahead; they struggled merely to survive.

This new atmosphere nourished frustrations. Middle-class whites, whose own aspirations for success were threatened by an unpredictable and unstable economy, raised questions that no one was ready to answer. Affirmative action, the policy that was seen by many as an opportunity for blacks to receive preferential treatment in jobs and educational opportunities, became ironically, a source of discontent rather than a solution to the problem. Whites raised legitimate questions: in a tight job market, should a more qualified white be forced to give up a job to a less-qualified black, even if the poorly qualified black was the victim of racially inspired inferior training? Blacks countered with the equally legitimate claim that they could not be held responsible for their own oppression, and that something had to be done in reparation for past wrongs to them as a people. No American institution, not even the United States Supreme Court, seemed either able or even willing to resolve that dilemma.

The seventies witnessed a revival of white racism and antiblack

MISSOURI'S POPULATION, 1900-1970

Year	Total	White	Negro	Other Races	Percent Negro
1970	4676501	4177495	480172	18834	10.3
1960	4319813	3922967	390853	5993	9.0
1950	3954653	3655593	297088	1972	7.5
1940	3784664	3539187	244386	1091	6.5
1930	3629367	3403876	223840	1651	6.2
1920	3404055	3225044	178241	770	5.2
1910	3293335	3134932	157452	951	4.8
1900	3106665	2944843	161234	588	5.2

(Source: 1970 Census of Population)

violence. In 1973, for example, a black couple's home in the Little Dixie town of Auxvasse was firebombed. The Ganaway family believed that their house was bombed because they were the first blacks to live in a previously all-white neighborhood. Likewise, the Ku Klux Klan has enjoyed a revival in the seventies. Mary E. Carr, the KKK's Grand Genie (head of the women's wing of the Klan) ran for mayor of Black Jack in 1979 and for city marshal in 1976 on an openly racist platform. In 1979 she received nearly 15 percent of the votes cast in the community. The Rev. James L. Betts, Grand Dragon (highest official) of the Ku Klux Klan in Missouri claimed a membership total of two thousand in 1979, although other membership estimates were much lower. In Centralia and other cities the Klan has openly appeared and sought permission to parade and hold rallies.

Persistent Segregation in the Seventies

Education. In 1975 the Missouri Human Rights Commission completed a study entitled "Integration in Missouri Public Schools: Faculty and Students Twenty Years After Brown." The report showed that throughout the state, faculties and students remained segregated. Especially in southeast Missouri, there were complaints that desegregation only meant the shutting down of black schools and the dismissal of black teachers. Within the school buildings, the report charged, segregation was maintained by class assignments and black pupils faced unfair and unequal disciplinary policies, some of which seemed aimed at forcing them to drop out of school. The report went on to state that 72 percent of the schools in St. Louis and 63 percent of

RATE OF UNEMPLOYMENT, 1970

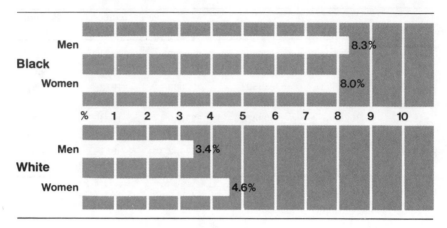

those in Kansas City had student bodies with 95 percent or more of one race.

By 1978, things were little better. In that year, the Missouri Department of Elementary and Secondary Education completed a survey of urban-metropolitan education in the state. More than 90 percent of the minority students still attended schools in minority school districts and the staff composition of the school districts generally reflected the districts' racial makeup. In short, nearly all the black students and staff were located in largely black school districts. In addition, the dropout rate was highest in the two largest minority school districts, St. Louis and Kansas City. The minority school districts generally received the least amount of money per pupil, although this varied from district to district. Perhaps most frustrating was the Department of Education's prediction that Missouri urban schools would become increasingly segregated in the 1980s.

As with the elementary and secondary schools, desegregation of Missouri's higher education facilities has been very slow. In 1979, a survey was conducted of the desegregation of several mid-Missouri universities. The only university to achieve any real degree of desegregation was the formerly all-black Lincoln University. Out of a total 2,085 undergraduates, there were 1,094 white students. On a faculty of 189 instructors, 101 were white. By contrast, the University of Missouri at Columbia had a black undergraduate student population of 575 out of a total student population of 17,152, less than 4 percent. Likewise, out

PLACE OF RESIDENCE, 1970

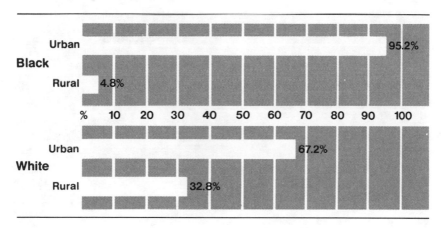

of a total faculty of 2,062, there were only 32 blacks, barely more than one percent.

Blacks and the Missouri Economy

The greatest problem facing black Missourians is unemployment. In 1970 the black population of Missouri stood at 480,172, or 10.3 percent of the total population of 4,676,501. Eighty-six percent of these blacks lived in the St. Louis and Kansas City areas. The income of the average black family was still 25 percent lower than that of the average white family, and approximately three times as many blacks as whites were unemployed.

St. Louis. As the decade of the seventies began, blacks in St. Louis found themselves in dire economic straits. There were approximately fifty-four thousand people in the city unemployed in 1970, 90 percent of whom were black. This situation was created in part by the fact that several large companies, such as the Chrysler Corporation, relocated their plants in suburban communities. With restrictive codes making housing more difficult for blacks to obtain in St. Louis County, the percentage of blacks working in such large plants was greatly reduced.

Housing was also a serious problem for blacks who remained in the city. Urban renewal programs often displaced many blacks. Between 1960 and 1965, for example, about six thousand new housing

AVERAGE (MEAN) FAMILY INCOME, 1970

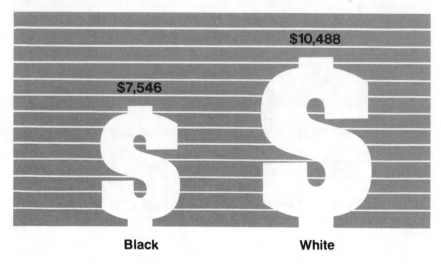

$10,488

$7,546

Black   **White**

units were built in St. Louis. At the same time more than twelve thousand units were destroyed by urban renewal and highway construction projects.

Despite these problems, the black business community in St. Louis
has remained active. C. W. Gates and I. O. Funderburg have provided
leadership as president and executive vice-president, respectively, of
the Gateway National Bank. The bank started in June of 1965 and before
the year's end had deposits of nearly $1.5 million. By 1971, the bank
had assets of $13 million. Gates was also interested in community
affairs. In 1966 he became the first black member of the St. Louis Board
of Police Commissioners. He also held a major interest in a local
radio station.

Perhaps one of the strongest traditions in black business is represented by the city's three black-owned weekly newspapers. The *St.
Louis American* and the *St. Louis Argus* each represent more than
fifty years of service by two newspaper families, the Sweets and the
Mitchells, respectively. The third weekly, the *St. Louis Sentinel,* is of
more recent origin.

One of the most creative black businesses in St. Louis is a corporation called Jeff-Vander-Lou, chartered in 1966. The organization
has made great progress in the rehabilitation of dwellings for area residents. Besides rehabilitating several hundred homes, Jeff-Vander-Lou,
under the leadership of Macler Shepard, has broken down a good deal
of union discrimination in the construction trade.

Three McDonald franchises are owned by Dr. Benjamin Davis. Other businesses include mortuaries, real estate firms, a casket factory, construction companies, repair shops, taverns, grocery stores, barbering and hair dressing parlors. Some black Missourians hold high managerial positions with large international and national corporations. Among these are Archie Price at Laclede Steel Company and James Webb, marketing manager of all forms of transportation for A. T. & T.

Kansas City. The employment problems of blacks in Kansas City are just as bad, if not worse, than those in St. Louis. The Federal Bureau of Labor Statistics estimated that the unemployment rate for non-whites (most of whom were black) in Kansas City for 1976 was 17.4 percent, even greater than St. Louis' 14.2 percent.

Most of Kansas City's black businesses remained service-oriented in the seventies. There are no black-owned banks or insurance companies as there are in St. Louis. McKinley Edmunds owns one of the largest black car dealerships in the country. Two successful black-owned businesses serve barbeque to Kansas Cityans: Ollie Gates & Sons and Arthur Bryant's. Everett P. O'Neal owns a tire company as well as a guard service and is involved in real estate. A public relations, advertising, and market research firm is owned by Inez Y. Kaiser. B. Lawrence Blankinship wholesales drugs and hair products. One of the most influential black-owned businesses is the newspaper, the *Kansas City Call.* The Black Economic Union, formed in 1967 by Curtis McClinton, Jr., a former player with the Kansas City Chiefs, has been successful. The Union created a Community Development Corporation in 1972 and encouraged the development of the Downtown East Industrial Park.

Drug stores, mortuaries, grocery stores, filling stations, real estate firms, house cleaning and window cleaning firms, contracting companies, barbering and hair dressing shops, and a building and loan company are among the other businesses owned by blacks in Kansas City.

Politics in the Seventies

The black population has been more successful in politics than in economics. One of the important sources of Kansas City's black political power is an organization called Freedom, Inc. This organization was established in 1962 by Leon Jordan and Bruce Watkins, two black businessmen. In that year the organization helped elect Leon Jordan a committeeman in Kansas City. Shortly thereafter, Bruce Watkins was elected to the city council. Freedom, Inc., had eight candidates running

Leon Jordan. (*Kansas City Star*)   Bruce Watkins campaign poster.
                                          (*Darryl C. Cook*)

in 1964, seven of whom won elective positions. By 1978, Freedom-
endorsed officials included four state representatives, two city
councilmen, three county legislators, one city judge, three school board
members, many members of municipal boards, and several committee-
men and committeewomen. In 1970 the organization suffered a blow
when its president, Leon Jordan, was assassinated. However, the organization continued with Bruce Watkins serving as president. Jordan's
widow, Orchid, won his seat in the State General Assembly. In 1976 the
organization suffered another setback when Harold Holliday, Sr., was
defeated in the Democratic primary in a bid for a state senate seat. Likewise, Bruce Watkins lost his bid to become mayor of Kansas City in
1979.

Missouri elected its first black senator, Theodore McNeal of St.

Senator Gwen Giles, first black woman elected state senator.

Louis, in 1960. In 1979, the state had two black senators, both from St. Louis: J. B. Banks and Gwen Giles. Only one black Missourian has been elected to the national legislature: current Congressman William Clay of St. Louis, who was first elected in 1968.

Blacks are increasingly included in policy-making positions of the state government. Out of thirty-two agencies, fifty-five blacks hold key appointments. Among them are Dr. Virginia H. Beard, Governor's Council on the Aging; Johnetta R. Haley, President, Board of Lincoln University Curators; Kelsey R. Beshears, Missouri Housing and Development Commission; Mary C. Jones, Statewide Health Coordinating Council; Leah Brock McCartney, Public Service Commission; Sherill Hunt, Director of Office of Economic Opportunity; Vernell E. Fuller, Director of the State Affirmative Action Office and adviser to the Gov-

Rep. William Clay, first black congressman from
Missouri. (*St. Louis American*)

ernor; and Alvin Brooks, Chairman of the Missouri Human Rights
Commission.

Other Outstanding Black Personalities

Greater access to educational facilities and a more liberal atmosphere in the state combined to allow a number of blacks to rise to
positions of prominence in a variety of fields in the sixties and seventies, despite persistent obstacles to their general progress.

Black ministers have always played a significant role in the struggle
for full citizenship. Among the well-known clergymen in the state have
been the Reverend Charles Briscoe of the Paseo Baptist Church of
Kansas City, who is also a former president of the school board; Father
Edward Warner, also a member of the school board; the Reverend John
Williams, pastor of the largest black Baptist church in Kansas City, and
the Reverends Earl Abel and Woody Hall. In Jefferson City, the Reverend
David Shipley of the Second Baptist Church made a name for himself
as the author of a history of black Baptists in Missouri. Prominent black
St. Louis ministers include the Reverend John Nance of the Washing-

State Representative DeVerne Calloway and
President Jimmy Carter. (St. Louis American)

ton Tabernacle, the Reverend Alvin Howard of St. James A.M.E. Church,
Dr. William Collins of Antioch Baptist Church, Dr. James Cummings of
Lane Tabernacle, and Fr. Chester Gaither of St. Matthew's Catholic
Church.

Black doctors are becoming increasingly numerous, although
there are still not enough of them to meet all of the health needs of the
urban communities. They are found in all aspects of medicine. Black
doctors in St. Louis include Drs. E. J. Taylor, Helen Nash, August Piper,
Samuel Westerfield, Jr., John W. Gladney, Herman Russell, James Whit-
tico, and Jerome Williams. In Kansas City, some of the more prominent
include Drs. Albert Crocker, Starks J. Williams, and Hayward Jackson.
In Jefferson City, there are Drs. William Ross, Charles Cooper, and
Elmer Jackson. More than fifty black physicians now serve the St.
Louis community, with a slightly lesser number serving in Kansas City.
One of the most recent controversies in St. Louis in the late seventies
was the attempt by the city to merge Homer G. Phillips Hospital with
City Hospital. Black groups argued that such a merger would not only
deprive northside blacks of needed medical services, but would also
result in the loss of more than one thousand health industry jobs at

St. Louis group gathers to protest the closing of Homer G. Phillips Hospital.
(*Darryl C. Cook*)

Homer Phillips. Despite their protests, the merger took place.

Blacks have steadily increased in the legal profession in the past few decades also. Most of Missouri's black lawyers practice in St. Louis and Kansas City. Some of them are Henry D. Espy, Joseph McDuffie, Nathan B. Young, Jr., Frankie Freeman, and Leonard Hughes, Jr. Hughes served as an Assistant Prosecutor in Kansas City and as an Assistant Attorney-General of the state of Missouri under Thomas Eagleton. Mrs. Freeman, a member of the United States Civil Rights Commission, was nominated in June 1979 by President Jimmy Carter to be the first Inspector-General of Health, Education and Welfare.

Black Missourians have also played important roles in education. Prominent among them in St. Louis are George Boyer Vashon, Sr. and Jr., Frank Lunsford Williams, Dr. James Scott, Dr. Samuel Shep-erd, Dr. Herman Dreer, and Bobette James. Dr. Robert Wheeler heads the Kansas City School system. Other prominent black educators in that city include Dr. A. Leedy Campbell and Dr. Girard Bryant. Dr.

Dr. Robert R. Wheeler, superintendent   Roy Wilkins receives check for
of schools, Kansas City.   NAACP. *(St. Louis American)*

Henry Givens served for a number of years as an Assistant Commissioner of the State Department of Education. Recently he was elected
president of the Harris-Stowe State College of St. Louis in 1979. Mention must be made of the presidents of Lincoln University who have
guided the destinies of black youth in search of higher education.
Among the recent presidents are Charles W. Florence, Sherman D.
Scruggs, Earl E. Dawson, Walter C. Daniels, and James Frank. In
outstate Missouri prominent black educators have included LeRoy
Shipley of Tipton, Alonzo Redmond of Jefferson City, and Muriel
and Elliott Battle of Columbia. Many blacks prominent in the civil
rights movement have come from Missouri. Perhaps the best known
are Roy Wilkins and Margaret Bush Wilson of the NAACP, and Leo
Bohannon of the Urban League.

Missouri blacks who have made contributions in the field of natural science include Dr. W. W. Dowdy and Dr. Charles Henry Turner,
nationally-recognized entomologists, and biologist Dr. Lloyd Fergu-

Margaret Bush Wilson, chairwoman, board
of directors, NAACP.

son and his son, Lloyd Ferguson, Jr., who was a cancer specialist at
the University of Chicago until his death in 1973. Drs. Moddie Taylor
and Willis Byrd are widely known as chemists. This fine tradition in
science is being carried forth by young scientists such as Drs. Herman
Miller and Nathan Cook of Lincoln University.

Missouri has produced a number of black writers, among them
Chester Himes of Jefferson City who wrote *Cotton Comes to Harlem*;
poet John Morris; author, poet, and playwright Maya Angelou; playwright Thomas D. Pawley; and short story writer Cecil A. Blue. Just
as importantly, in the last decade blacks have moved in increasing
numbers into responsible positions as broadcasters and news jour-
nalists. In Kansas City, Corrice Collins, Brenda Williams, and Gayle
King have established themselves in the broadcasting field, as have
Julius Hunter, Dianne White, Robin Smith, and Michel Brown in
the St. Louis area.

Other black Missourians have gained recognition in the field of
social science. Drs. Sherman Savage and Arvarh Strickland are
well-known historians, as is Julia Davis, who taught for years in the
St. Louis school district. Dr. Oliver C. Cox, a longtime Lincoln Uni-

Felicia Weathers, great soprano
opera singer. (St. Louis American)

Grace Bumbry, opera star.
(St. Louis American)

Dr. Thomasina Talley (Greene),
concert pianist.

5th Dimension have some native Missourians
among their number. *(St. Louis American)*

versity sociologist, achieved an international reputation for works
such as *Caste, Class and Race*.

Among the many outstanding social workers are Frankie Spearman, Ina Lindsey, and Chester Stovall.

In the field of classical music, Eugene Haynes, Thomasina Talley
Greene, O. Anderson Fuller, O'Hara Spearman, Kenneth Billups, and
Lawrence Kimbrough all add lustre to Missouri's artistic life. On the
stage, classical and operatic stars such as Felicia Weathers and Grace
Bumbry have won accolades from worldwide audiences for their
artistry. It is a sad commentary upon American society that many of
these black performers had to be acclaimed in Europe before being
accepted at home.

Current day entertainers Redd Foxx, LaWanda Page, and Dick
Gregory all started in Missouri.

These persons have achieved success despite the obstacles that
being black have created for them. Their accomplishments stand as
an inspiration to young people, giving both black and white youth

Missourian Redd Foxx of *Sanford and Son* TV fame.
(*St. Louis American*)

a sense of pride in the knowledge that their ancestors were co-builders of Missouri civilization.

The accomplishments of black Missourians alone will not solve the problem of racism. Neither will the emergence of a strong black middle-class, represented by these people. The masses of blacks are ill-fed, under-employed, poorly-housed, and undereducated. The answer lies in a realization that black and white life is so intertwined that the history of one is incomplete without the other. If that is true of our past, it is even more true of the present and the future. No one group can live to the exclusion or detriment of any other group.

Gains have been made, but the victory has not yet been won. The struggle must go on until all persons, regardless of race, creed, color, nationality, or sex share equally in the opportunities and obligations of democracy. The future demands that we recognize these facts and that we live accordingly, recognizing and utilizing the talent and intrinsic worth of all men and women. Only the future will tell whether or not we can measure up to the task.

SUGGESTED READINGS

As yet very little published material exists for the period 1968 to the present. The Missouri Commission on Human Rights' *Annual Reports* and the commission's newsletter, *Progress* should be examined. In addition, Rex Campbell and Thomas E. Baker, *The Negro in Missouri—1970* (Jefferson City, 1972), should be looked at for an analysis of the racial characteristics of the Missouri population based on the U.S. Census of 1970. Thomas E. Baker and Rex Campbell, *Race and Residence in Missouri Cities* (Jefferson City, 1971), provides an analysis of continued housing discrimination in ten Missouri cities based on the 1970 U.S. Census. Two reports in 1979 by the Missouri Advisory Committee to the United States Commission on Civil Rights are quite helpful. They are *Race Relations in the "Kingdom" of Callaway* and *Race Relations in Cooper County, Missouri—1978*.

The problems of bringing true integration to Missouri schools is examined in David Henderson, *Integration in Missouri Public Schools* (Jefferson City, 1974), and in the Missouri Department of Elementary and Secondary Education, *A Study of Urban-Metropolitan Education in Missouri* (Jefferson City, 1978).

Useful information on the economic life of the St. Louis black population can be found in "St. Louis," *Black Enterprise*, II (August 1971). The economic and political situation of blacks in Kansas City, Missouri, is well covered by Jeanne Allyson Fox, "In Kansas City, Missouri, Economic Development Plays Catch up to Political Clout," *Black Enterprise*, VIII (March 1978).

Missouri's Black Heritage

Appendix

Appendix

Missouri Black Legislators

U. S. Congress

House of Representatives

William L. Clay *(Democrat)*   First district
St. Louis City *(Elected November 5, 1968; reelected*
November 3, 1970; November 7, 1972; November 5,
1974; November 2, 1976; November, 1978.

State Representatives

1921-1922   51st General Assembly

Walthall M. Moore *(Republican)*   Sixth district
St. Louis City

1925-1926   53rd General Assembly

Walthall M. Moore *(Republican)*   Third district
St. Louis City

1927-1928   54th General Assembly

John A. Davis *(Republican)*   Third district
St. Louis City

Walthall M. Moore *(Republican)*   Third district
St. Louis City

1929-1930   55th General Assembly
Walthall M. Moore *(Republican)*   Third district
St. Louis City

1931-1932   56th General Assembly
Frank W. Clegg, *(Republican)*   Third district
St. Louis City

1943-1944   62nd General Assembly
Edwin F. Kenwil *(Democrat)*   Fourth district
St. Louis City

1945-1946   63rd General Assembly
James McKinley Neal, *(Democrat)*   Fourth district
Jackson County

1947-1948   64th General Assembly
J. Clayborne Bush *(Republican)*   Seventeenth district
St. Louis City

William A. Massingale *(Democrat)*   Eleventh district
St. Louis City

Josiah C. Thomas *(Republican)*   Tenth district
St. Louis City

1949-1950   65th General Assembly
William A. Cole *(Democrat)*   Tenth district
St. Louis City

John Wilson Greene *(Democrat)*   Seventeenth district
St. Louis City

Walter V. Lay *(Democrat)*   Eleventh district
St. Louis City *(elected 1948)*

James McKinley Neal *(Democrat)*   Fourth district
Jackson County

1951-1952   66th General Assembly
John Wilson Greene *(Democrat)*   Seventeenth district
St. Louis City

Walter V. Lay *(Democrat)*   Eleventh district
St. Louis City

James McKinley Neal *(Democrat)*   Fourth district
Jackson County (1946, 1948, 1950)

LeRoy Tyus *(Democrat)*   Tenth district
St. Louis City

1953-1954   67th General Assembly

John Wilson Greene *(Democrat)*   Seventeenth district
St. Louis City *(first elected 1948 and reelected
1950 and 1952)*

Walter V. Lay *(Democrat)*   Eleventh district
St. Louis City *(elected in 1948, 1950 and
reelected 1952)*

James McKinley Neal, *(Democrat)*   Fourth district
Jackson County *(elected 1946, was reelected
1948, 1950 and 1952)*

LeRoy Tyus *(Democrat)*   Tenth district
St. Louis City

1955-1956   68th General Assembly

John Wilson Greene *(Democrat)*   Seventeenth district
St. Louis City

J. McKinley Neal *(Democrat)*   Fourth district
Jackson County

James P. Troupe, Sr. *(Democrat)*   Eleventh district
St. Louis City

LeRoy Tyus *(Democrat)*   Tenth district
St. Louis City

1957-1958   69th General Assembly

J. McKinley Neal *(Democrat)*   Fourth district
Jackson County

James P. Troupe, Sr. *(Democrat)*   Eleventh district
St. Louis City

LeRoy Tyus *(Democrat)*   Tenth district
St. Louis City

Henry W. Wheeler *(Democrat)*   Seventeenth district
St. Louis City *(elected 1956)*

1959-1960   70th General Assembly

J. McKinley Neal *(Democrat)*   Fourth district
Jackson County

James P. Troupe, Sr. *(Democrat)*   Eleventh district
St. Louis City

LeRoy Tyus *(Democrat)*   Tenth district
St. Louis City

Henry W. Wheeler *(Democrat)*   Seventeenth district
St. Louis City

1961-1962   71st General Assembly

State Senators

Theodore D. McNeal (Democrat)   Seventh district
St. Louis City (elected 1960)

State Representatives

James McKinley Neal (Democrat)   Fourth district
Jackson County

Rev. William Wright (Democrat)   Eleventh district
St. Louis City

Hugh J. White (Democrat)   Sixteenth district
St. Louis City

Henry W. Wheeler (Democrat)   Seventeenth district
St. Louis City

1963-1964   72nd General Assembly

State Senator

Theodore D. McNeal (Democrat)   Fourth district
St. Louis City

State Representatives

James McKinley Neal (Democrat)   Fourth district
Jackson County

James P. Troupe, Sr. (Democrat)   Ninth district
St. Louis City

Hugh J. White (Democrat)   Tenth district
St. Louis City

*DeVerne Lee Calloway (Democrat)   Thirteenth district
St. Louis City

John Conley, Jr. (Democrat)   Fifteenth district
St. Louis City

*First black woman representative.

1965-1966   73rd General Assembly

State Senator

Theodore D. McNeal (Democrat)   Fourth district
St. Louis City

State Representatives

Henry Ross, (Democrat)   Second district
Jackson County

Harold L. Holliday, *(Democrat)*   Fifth district
Jackson County

Leon M. Jordan, *(Democrat)*   Fourth district
Jackson County

James P. Troupe, Sr., *(Democrat)*   Ninth district
St. Louis City

Raymond Howard *(Democrat)*   Tenth district
St. Louis City

DeVerne Lee Calloway, *(Democrat)*   Thirteenth district
St. Louis City

John Conley, Jr., *(Democrat)*   Fifteenth district
St. Louis City

1967-1968   74th General Assembly

State Senator

Theodore D. McNeal *(Democrat)*   Fourth district
St. Louis City

State Representatives

Henry Ross *(Democrat)*   Tenth district
Jackson County

Leon M. Jordan *(Democrat)*   Eleventh district
Jackson County

James W. Spencer *(Democrat)*   Thirteenth district
Jackson County

Harold L. Holliday *(Democrat)*   Fourth district
Jackson County

James P. Troupe, Sr. *(Democrat)*   Fifty-third district
St. Louis City

Raymond Howard, *(Democrat)*   Fifty-fourth district
St. Louis City

DeVerne Lee Calloway *(Democrat)*   Seventieth district
St. Louis City

Elsa Debra Hill *(Democrat)*   Seventy-first district
St. Louis City

Franklin Payne, *(Democrat)*   Seventy-third district
St. Louis City

Johnnie S. Aikens *(Democrat)*   Seventy-fourth district
St. Louis City

John Conley, Jr. *(Democrat)*   Seventy-fifth district
St. Louis City

Russell Goward *(Democrat)*   Seventy-sixth district
St. Louis City

1969-1970   75th General Assembly

State Senators

Theodore D. McNeal *(Democrat)*   Fourth district
St. Louis City

Raymond Howard *(Democrat)*   Fifth district
St. Louis City

State Representatives

Henry Ross, *(Democrat)*   Tenth district
Jackson County

Leon M. Jordan *(Democrat)*   Eleventh district
Jackson County

Herman A. Johnson, *(Democrat)*   Thirteenth district
Jackson County

Harold L. Holliday *(Democrat)*   Fourteenth district
Jackson County

James P. Troupe, Sr., *(Democrat)*   Fifty-third district
St. Louis City

J. B. (Jet) Banks, *(Democrat)*   Fifty-fourth district
St. Louis City

DeVerne Lee Calloway *(Democrat)*   Seventieth district
St. Louis City

Nathaniel J. Rivers, *(Democrat)*   Seventy-first district
St. Louis City

Fred Williams, *(Democrat)*   Seventy-second district
St. Louis City

Franklin Payne *(Democrat)*   Seventy-third district
St. Louis City

Johnnie S. Aikens *(Democrat)*   Seventy-fourth district
St. Louis City

LeRoy Malcolm *(Democrat)*   Seventy-fifth district
St. Louis City

Russell Goward *(Democrat)*   Seventy-sixth district
St. Louis City

1971-1972   76th General Assembly

State Senators

Franklin Payne *(Democrat)*   Fourth district
St. Louis City

Raymond Howard. *(Democrat)*   Fifth district
St. Louis City

State Representatives

Henry Ross *(Democrat)* Jackson County	Tenth district
Orchid I. Jordan *(Democrat)* Jackson County	Eleventh district
Herman A. Johnson *(Democrat)* Jackson County	Thirteenth district
Harold Holliday. *(Democrat)* Jackson County	Fourteenth district
James P. Troupe, Sr. *(Democrat)* St. Louis City	Fifty-third district
J. B. (Jet) Banks *(Democrat)* St. Louis City	Fifty-fourth district
DeVerne Lee Calloway *(Democrat)* St. Louis City	Seventieth district
Nathaniel J. Rivers, *(Democrat)* St. Louis City	Seventy-first district
Fred Williams *(Democrat)* St. Louis City	Seventy-second district
Fred E. Brown *(Democrat)* St. Louis City	Seventy-third district
Johnnie S. Aikens, *(Democrat)* St. Louis City	Seventy-fourth district
John Conley, Jr.. *(Democrat)* St. Louis City	Seventy-fifth district
Russell Goward, *(Democrat)* St. Louis City	Seventy-sixth district

1973-1974   77th General Assembly

State Senators

Franklin Payne, *(Democrat)* St. Louis City	Fourth district
Raymond Howard *(Democrat)* St. Louis City	Fifth district

State Representatives

Orchid I. Jordan. *(Democrat)* Jackson County	Twenty-fifth district
Harold L. Holliday *(Democrat)* Jackson County	Twenty-sixth district

Phillip B. Curls, *(Democrat)* Jackson County	Twenty-eighth district
Leo McKamey *(Democrat)* Jackson County	Thirty-sixth district
Raymond Quarles *(Democrat)* St. Louis City	Sixty-third district
Russell Goward *(Democrat)* St. Louis City	Sixty-fifth district
Johnnie S. Aikens, *(Democrat)* St. Louis City	Sixty-sixth district
James M. Carrington *(Democrat)* St. Louis City	Sixty-seventh district
Fred Williams *(Democrat)* St. Louis City	Seventy-eighth district
Nathaniel J. Rivers *(Democrat)* St. Louis City	Seventy-ninth district
J. B. (Jet) Banks *(Democrat)* St. Louis City	Eightieth district
DeVerne Lee Calloway *(Democrat)* St. Louis City	Eighty-first district
Harold Martin *(Democrat)* St. Louis City	Eighty-second district

1975-1976   78th General Assembly

State Senators

Franklin Payne *(Democrat)* St. Louis City	Fourth district
Raymond Howard *(Democrat)* St. Louis City	Fifth district

State Representatives

Orchid I. Jordan *(Democrat)* Jackson County	Twenty-fifth district
Harold L. Holliday *(Democrat)* Jackson County	Twenty-sixth district
Phillip B. Curls, *(Democrat)* Jackson County	Twenty-eighth district
Leo McKamey *(Democrat)* Jackson County	Thirty-sixth district
Raymond Quarles *(Democrat)* St. Louis City	Sixty-third district
Russell Goward *(Democrat)* St. Louis City	Sixty-fifth district

Johnnie S. Aikens *(Democrat)*   Sixty-sixth district
St. Louis City

James M. Carrington, *(Democrat)*   Sixty-seventh district
St. Louis City

Fred Williams, *(Democrat)*   Seventy-eighth district
St. Louis City

Nathaniel J. Rivers *(Democrat)*   Seventy-ninth district
St. Louis City

*J. B. (Jet) Banks, *(Democrat)*   Eightieth district
St. Louis City

DeVerne Lee Calloway *(Democrat)*   Eighty-first district
St. Louis City

Roscoe L. McCrary *(Democrat)*   Eighty-second district
St. Louis City

*J. B. Banks–House Officer. Assistant Majority Floor Leader.

1977-1978   79th General Assembly

State Senators

Franklin Payne *(Democrat)*   Fourth district
St. Louis City

J. B. (Jet) Banks *(Democrat)*   Fifth district
St. Louis City

State Representatives

Orchid I. Jordan *(Democrat)*   Twenty-fifth district
Jackson County

Alan D. Wheat *(Democrat)*   Twenty-sixth district
Jackson County

Phillip B. Curls *(Democrat)*   Twenty-eighth district
Jackson County

Leo McKamey *(Democrat)*   Thirty-sixth district
Jackson County

Raymond Quarles *(Democrat)*   Sixty-third district
St. Louis City

Russell Goward *(Democrat)*   Sixty-fifth district
St. Louis City

Johnnie S. Aikens *(Democrat)*   Sixty-sixth district
St. Louis City

James M. Carrington *(Democrat)*   Sixty-seventh district
St. Louis City

Fred Williams *(Democrat)*   Seventy-eighth district
St. Louis City

Nathaniel J. Rivers *(Democrat)*   Seventy-ninth district
St. Louis City

Robert L. Walker *(Democrat)*   Eightieth district
St. Louis City

DeVerne Lee Calloway *(Democrat)*   Eighty-first district
St. Louis City

Roscoe L. McCrary *(Democrat)*   Eighty-second district
St. Louis City

1979-1980   80th General Assembly

State Senators

*Gwen Giles *(Democrat)*   Fourth district
St. Louis City

J. B. Banks *(Democrat)*   Fifth district
St. Louis City

State Representatives

Nathaniel J. Rivers *(Democrat)*   Seventy-ninth district
St. Louis City

Fred Williams *(Democrat)*   Seventy-eighth district
St. Louis City

Russell Goward *(Democrat)*   Sixty-fifth district
St. Louis City

Charles Troupe *(Democrat)*   Sixty-third district
St. Louis City

Phil Curls *(Democrat)*   Twenty-eighth district
Jackson County

Alan Wheat *(Democrat)*   Twenty-sixth district
Jackson County

Leo McKamey *(Democrat)*   Thirty-sixth district
Jackson County

Orchid Jordan *(Democrat)*   Twenty-eighth district
Jackson County

DeVerne Calloway *(Democrat)*   Eighty-first district
St. Louis City

Johnnie Aikens *(Democrat)*   Sixty-sixth district
St. Louis City

Elbert Walton *(Democrat)*   Eightieth district
St. Louis City

Billy Boykins *(Democrat)*   Eighty-second district
St. Louis City

James Carrington *(Democrat)*   Sixty-seventh district
St. Louis City

*First black woman elected to State Senate.

Index